G000300378

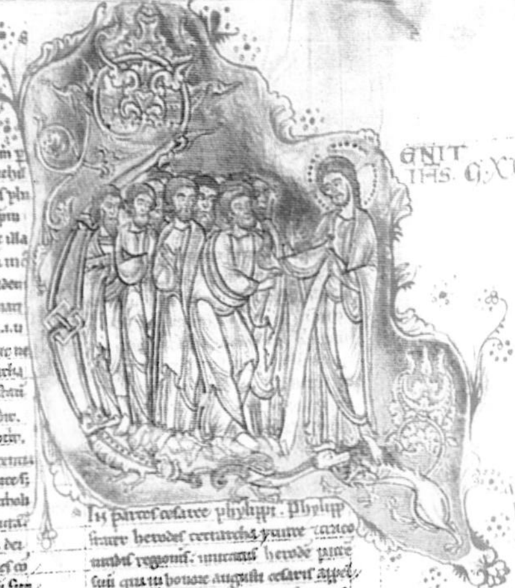

ABBOTSBURY

Sketched in Mist and Sunlight

Nigel Melville

Odun Books
1999

For Sue

CONTENTS

Introduction

Sometimes, as you come over the hill from Bridport, the mist lies over the land, *"as though a bed were preparing for a cloud-gathering god"* as Llewellyn Powys once described the Dorset coast, and only the Chapel and the tops of the hills stand out above the surface. That's how the Abbotsbury story seems to me ~ a brief glimpse, now and then, of a moment in time, then the mists close in again, and you are left to wonder how it all affected the people who lived here.

This is not a guide book, nor a history book; I have simply tried to catch in words what makes Abbotsbury different from other Dorset villages, and I have my doubts about how well I might have done: in the first few months after my wife and I came here to run the Wheelwrights Tea Rooms, we lost count of the number of times people used the word "magic" in trying to describe Abbotsbury, and you can't put magic down in black and white.

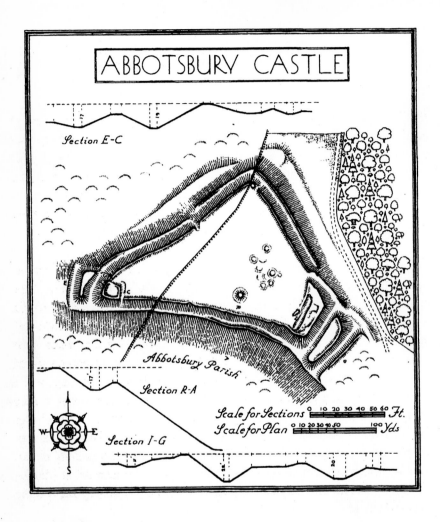

ABBOTSBURY CASTLE

Section E-C

Abbotsbury Parish

Section R-A

Scale for Sections   0 10 20 30 40 50 60 *Ft.*

Scale for Plan   0 10 20 30 40 50   100 *Yds*

Section I-G

One

The Hill Fort and the Raiders

If all our yesterdays were a single day, and Jesus Christ were born at noon, the first people to live in Abbotsbury arrived at about 6.00am, but the Abbey wasn't founded until shortly after 1.00pm and was suppressed within half an hour, while we would be looking back on it all from the vantage point of 2.00pm in the early afternoon.   That's how long ago it all started; even the oldest elements of what we think of as Abbotsbury history is only a fraction of the total span of settlement here.

Where it started was on top of the hill as you drive here from Bridport. Turn left at the sign which says "Ashley Chase only", and park in the little lay-by.   A few steps up a narrow path, and you're on the edge of the original Abbotsbury.   Ten acres of multivallate fort ~ "multivallate" meaning "several ramparts and ditches", the idea being that when your enemies (and there were plenty of them) called, you could stand on top of the first rampart and throw stones at them as they tried to climb up, and if that didn't work, there would be reserves of people and stones hidden ready behind the next rampart, both of which would come as a surprise to the invader.   If throwing stones seems a poor form of defence, remember David and Goliath, and that Chesil Beach is a handy munitions dump. The archaeologists turned up 40,000 Chesil pebbles stockpiled at Maiden Castle, carried all that way by the primitive people who nearly saw off the Roman legions.

Not that life was all that brutal in Abbotsbury Castle.   For the most part, the first villagers here grew their crops, looked after their animals, raised their children and buried their dead in an orderly manner.   Yet the hill fort still hides whatever secrets it holds, for it has never been excavated, but if

5

the studies on Maiden Castle and the other sites which cluster so closely across these hills are any guide, the people who lived on our hilltop were not wholly savage: they had the techniques, the tools, and the social organisation to clear the area of woodland, they were sufficiently skilled and settled to graze livestock, spin fleece into wool and weave it into cloth, and build their houses of stone in such a way that the entrance passages were sheltered from the prevailing wind. And they buried their dead.

If I keep on about that, it's because the 20 or more burial mounds in Abbotsbury parish offer the best evidence of the society that did the burying; from the mounds come the stone axe heads, the bronze knives and the iron implements that give their names to the Ages which we glibly use as labels to catalogue centuries of civilization ~ the "Bronze Age" lasted as long as the spell from the Roman invasion of Britain to the English Civil War, yet we lump it with the Stone and Iron Ages as "prehistoric" as if we are the only people who have ever mattered. No doubt the folk who built the hill fort would flounder if they came back to our time ~ but would we fare any better if everything we needed had to be grown, reared, or made by hand, and everything we needed to learn had to be memorised ?

It was the Roman occupation that began the real changes in Abbotsbury. By then, about a decade after the Crucifixion, the people of the hill fort had begun to move down into the valley where the village now stands. Their farms had become rather more like the countryside we see today, and no doubt they fished off the beach, as their descendants were to do until quite recent times. Peace and tranquillity came at a price, as the skeletons of the defenders of Maiden Castle so eloquently tell, but the scars were eventually covered by assimilation into the "Romano-British" community. Of course, that's shorthand for something that took several generations: maybe historians will look back on us, decide that we became "Anglo-European" around the turn of the second millennium, and put us equally glibly and equally inaccurately in just such a neat little slot.

6

Neat or not, the Romano-British settlement didn't have it all its own way, and the hill fort above the Bridport road had its uses over the next few hundred years. Again, I stress that a "few hundred" should not trip so easily on to the page: the period from the departure of the Romans to Orc's foundation of the Abbey is every bit as long as the period from Henry VIII's desecration of the Abbey buildings to the present day. Sometimes, as you walk round the village, the old buildings make their history all seem like yesterday ~ but it wasn't yesterday, it was all a very long time ago. And the people who had to pick up their belongings and run to the security of the hill fort time and time again, as invaders landed in wave after wave on the beach must have thought it a very long time indeed.

Four centuries after they arrived, the Romans pulled the protective legions back to the sunny, if beleaguered, south, and left our ancestors to their own devices. The isolated villas were the first to fall derelict, then the great straight roads and the legions' signalling posts, until finally the towns themselves lost all semblance of Imperial outposts. Time for another occupation, as a near-contemporary monk described how the "loathsome hordes" swept on to shores like the Chesil Beach "like dark swarms of worms." The "Dark Ages" rolled on as the native British fought the German Saxons for control of the southern coast, but out of them came the kingdom we know as Wessex, and into Wessex came the missionaries from Rome, building their religious houses, including the great monastery at Glastonbury which held land here in Abbotsbury by the gift of King Athelstan, a royal connection which may account for the belief that our village was the chosen place of retreat for the Saxon kings. On the other hand, our little valley is at the heart of the Wessex kingdom which ran from Hampshire to the Cornish border: we may simply have been chosen by the Royal family of the day for just the same reasons as bring so many people here a thousand years later ~ seclusion, a mild climate, fantastic views of land and sea, and a general air of well-being. Who knows ?

What brings us to the end of the beginning is a passing reference which is generally written off as a romantic fancy. William Coker was for years held to be the 18th century author of Dorset's first guidebook until it was discovered that Thomas Gerard actually wrote it in the 1620s: it was Gerard who remarked that in Abbotsbury *"if you will beleeve a Relation in the Register of that Monasterie, was built, in the verie Infancie of Christianitie amongst the Britons, a Church to St Peter, by Bertufus an holie Priest unto whom the same Saint had often appeared ..."*

Set aside the bizarre claim that in one of his appearances St Peter handed over a charter he had prepared earlier in his own hand, and you are still left with some solid facts. If you take the birth of Christianity in England as 597AD, when St Augustine landed in Kent, then the conversion of Wessex and the appointment of a bishop at Dorchester only 40 years later is surely in the "verie infancie" of the new religion. And when the Abbey was founded four centuries later it was dedicated to the same St Peter who had already named our village "Abodesbyry." Which leads one to ask why a village without an Abbey should be called "the Abbot's Village." And why, when the Abbey was a Norman foundation, are there some oddly powerful faces gazing impassively down from the houses where they have been relocated, which the experts say are Saxon or maybe Celtic, and thus much much older than anything built by the Benedictines ? Something holy was established here in this valley when the original villagers moved down from that hillside fort. Quite what it was might become clearer in the next chapter.

Two

The King's Man

We are all Europeans now, so we are told. But we've been here before.
In the space of forty years at the start of this millennium, we had three
kings in a row, who were, in turn, Saxon, Danish, and Norman. The fact
that two of them shared the same Norman queen merely adds to the
complications.

But let's go back several hundred years from 1000AD to the elusive
Bertufus. If he built his little church here in the 7th century, things might
have seemed settled then, but the next wave of invaders was to be even
worse than the last. According to Roy Strong, *"the Vikings terrified the
Saxons as much as they themselves had terrified the Britons centuries
before"*, and if that sounds like civilised hindsight, Strong quotes the
Anglo-Saxon Chronicle's accounts of invasions every ten years or so.
"Invasion", don't forget, is shorthand for the squalid murder, looting and
destruction which today we call "ethnic cleansing". Wessex alone held
out against the invaders with any success (which again suggests why the
Saxon kings favoured Abbotsbury as a retreat), until Alfred settled the
matter in 878 from his island fort at Athelney on the Somerset levels, only
50 miles from here, giving both land and people the breathing space
needed to ensure that no further invasions would succeed, at least in this
part of the country.

Did those invasions include Abbotsbury? Of course they did: Gerard's
account of the foundation of the Abbey in Norman times adds that there
had been a church here, *"longe before built, but then decayed and
forsaken by reason the rovers from the Sea often infested it."*

Alfred's legacy of security may have been false, for the Northern invaders

9

slowly annexed great swathes of England to their Scandinavian empire: our relationship to the rest of Europe was just as ambivalent in 1000AD as it is on the brink of 2000.

The key figures in bringing the Abbey to Abbotsbury weren't men, but women. To start with, there's French-born Queen Emma, mother of Edward the Confessor, great-aunt of William the Conqueror and one-time second wife of the Saxon Ethelred the Unready. "Unready", by the way, is a curious nickname, for Ethelred means "noble counsel", while "Unraed", means "no counsel": centuries later, one of his heirs would be similarly described as "the wisest fool in Christendom". On the death of her husband and the defeat of her stepson who had briefly succeeded him, Queen Emma duly did what was expected of her, and married the Dane who had taken over the south of England just as he had subdued the north.

"Subdued" is another clinical euphemism. Cnut the Dane was a bloodthirsty specimen from a race which counted heroism by the gallons of enemy blood spilt and the acreage of land set aflame. Yet this is the same man who turned himself inside out to become a sober, if over-zealous, lawgiver, and brought a short and fragile peace to what was beginning to be recognisable as one country. Cnut may be better known as the King Canute who is ridiculed for trying to stop the sea in its tracks. Actually, he was quite sensibly showing his more unctuous courtiers that there are things even a King can't do, and legend has it that he used Chesil Beach for the lesson.

Among Queen Emma's ladies, it is said, was one Tola who already owned land in Dorset (she's the Tol- in Tolpuddle): we can only guess how she, as a Norman, came to be married to Orc, who was a servant of this Danish-born King. Anyway, Orc was close to the King, thus close to the Queen, and close to her circle. Whether or not he was a pious character, he must have been a shrewd and diplomatic soul to have not only survived the bloodbath which lay between the death of Cnut and the succession of Edward the Confessor, but to have found office again under that saintly ruler. Gerard says he was a "houscarle" to the King, but that doesn't tell us a lot about him. Other writers describe him as a steward, a seneschal, an "oeconomus", or a "domestic or menial servant." I doubt it: in the Scots clan system, the Chief's carles were closer to being bodyguards, and a recent book describes the house-carles of the Norman Kings as being *"the nearest equivalent to a police force: they administered his laws and enforced his royal authority."* This Orc, praised by his King for his "amiable fidelity and willing mind", did a lot more for his master than decant his wine and warm his slippers. Take a look at the Bayeux Tapestry ~ those men with battle axes are house-carles.

Anyway, back to the beginnings of the Abbey: Cnut re-invented himself for the same reason he married Ethelred's widow, namely to boost his authority and improve his image, but something of the guilt that perhaps he felt about earlier days may have lain on his conscience ~ *"This fleeting life is so full of worldly miseries and by various imperfections consumed and wasted by trouble that in cases of premature death very many, alas! are dragged unprepared into eternity ..."* A strange way to preface a gift of land from a one-time warlord to his chief of staff, even in the uneasy days of 1024. Gift of land it was, though; seven hides in and around Portesham, and a generous one, for seven hides was about 850 acres. But, to an incomer like me, the boundaries of the King's gift don't read like anywhere I've seen on road signs here. Wherever it all was, the deed of gift was significant enough for the King to have it witnessed by an Archbishop, 4 Bishops, 3 Dukes, 5 Abbots, 3 Priests and no less than 20 "ministers", though whether of state or religion isn't stated.

Cnut's gift to Orc is important because it led to him and his wife Tola giving land in Abbotsbury to the "decayed and forsaken" church in the valley. Thus it was that in 1044, by which time Cnut had been dead eight years and his children had done their best to demolish all he had created, Orc, now serving Edward the Confessor and himself beginning perhaps to think a little about being "dragged unprepared into eternity", set about creating a proper Benedictine Abbey here.

I use that word "proper" because there are two theories about the start of the Abbey; *either* that 1044 was the start date, *or* that it was the date when an earlier community, established by Orc in 1026, was up-graded: it all turns on whether you consider a group of secular canons ("ordinary" priests rather than monks belonging to a recognised order) can be classed as a monastery. Either way, by 1044, the Benedictines were here, and were here to stay for a tiny fraction under 500 years. Not a bad record, and one that the current owners won't match for another 35 years. Nor was the monastery Orc's only gift to the village: he founded a guild (a charitable brotherhood, fore-runner of the Friendly Society movement), at much the same time as he set up the Abbey. The charter establishing the guild, like the deed giving the land, is still to be seen in the County Record Office in Dorchester. As I said at the outset, these things are comparatively recent events in the village's history.

That word "bloodbath" cropped up earlier, suggesting that the early days of the Abbey here were not entirely peaceful; when Duke William ordered the registration of property that we call the Domesday Book, some 40 years after the foundation of the Abbey, another formidable lady flashes briefly into focus. Hadwidia Fitz Grip laid claim (often illegally) to 30,000 acres of land, not a bad holding when you reckon that the King and Queen together claimed less than 140,000, and that the Abbey at its height held only 2,500 acres in Abbotsbury. The trouble was, according to the careful civil servants of 1086, *"To this manor (i.e. to the Abbey) belongs one hide, which in King Edward's time was for the sustenance of the monks. Hugh Fitz Grip took this unjustly and kept it: and his wife still keeps possession of it by force."* Petticoat rule was clearly a force to be reckoned with in turn-of-the-millennium Abbotsbury.

In between the Abbey's foundation and the writing of the Domesday Book, that original deed of gift to Orc was confirmed by Edward the Confessor, who matched Cnut's original gift with a grant of land and significant rights that were valuable enough to have been regularly confirmed by one king after another ~ which is my cowardly way of saying that I haven't a

12

clue what "sac, soc, tol" or "infangenthief" might mean in Anglo-Saxon or mediaeval Latin, never mind in everyday English.

Whatever all the antiquated terms meant, the Abbey had already grown enough to hold those 2,500 acres within its first 50 years, together with two mills, and at least 36 acres of meadow land, pasture and woodland, worked by over 60 labourers of one sort of another.   Quite a thriving community, and all of it up and running not long after the Battle of Hastings.   The tragedy, though, is that we'll never know much more than that about the early days of the Abbey, because so many of its records were lost when the Strangways house ~ that's a later story ~ was so stupidly blown up in the Civil War.   Gerard saw them not long before they went up in flames, just like he saw Orc's tomb, but as Hutchins, the classic historian of Dorset complains rather self-righteously, he recorded only "a legend and a few obscure hints".   Everything else was lost.

Well, not quite everything.   In the Oxfordshire library of Sir Paul Getty, there is a small 180-page book, bound in wood covered with deer skin, with a note in Latin on the back page to say that "this book belongs to God and the Church of St Peter and Paul the Apostles at Abbotsbury". This is *"In Unum ex Quatuor"*, more commonly called the *Zacharias Chrysopolitanus*, a commentary on a commentary on a commentary of the four Gospels, written around 1140 and copied by a monk of Winchester or perhaps of Abbotsbury itself, and richly illuminated with colourful scenes, fantastic animals and gloriously ornamental lettering.

"A commentary on a commentary ...." ?   A scholar called Tatian wrote a book in Greek, called the *Diatessaron,* all about the similarities and differences between the Gospels; then another scholar called Victor of Capua wrote a Latin version of Tatian's book, and Zacharias, a monk of Besançon in France, at one time called Chrysopolis, wrote this book about Victor's book about Tatian's book about the Gospels.   People talk about mediaeval scholars arguing over how many angels could dance on the head of a pin; you can see what they mean.

13

For such a little book, it's done a lot of travelling: at the time of writing, it's on show at the Pierpont Morgan Library in New York. Copied from the French edition, our *Zacharias* may have been well used by our monks (lots of pages are missing), but at some time in the 16th century it was sold to a farmer at Elworth, just up the road from here, and from there it went to Dewlish, just beyond Dorchester, where it stayed until 1925.

It then found its way to the Chester Beatty collection, from which it was sold, in 1933, for the princely sum of £490 to the library of a Californian seminary, who held it for over 50 years before putting it on the market in 1987. Listed with a guide price of £200,000 to £250,000, it sailed past the target, finishing up well into seven figures. What might the rest of the Abbey library have fetched ? And what happened to the other Abbotsbury book thought by a former vicar to have been on the Chester Beatty sale list in 1933 ? The one described as the Closworth Missal, including a Crucifixion scene which might, according to the then Earl of Ilchester, who had seen the book, have been modelled on the view from the top of our hills ? According to the British Library, the V & A and the top London antiquarian booksellers, it doesn't appear in the Chester Beatty list nor in the standard work on mediaeval monastic manuscripts. The mists seem to have gathered once more.

Three

The Monks of St Benedict

Think "monks" these days, and you tend to think "Cadfael", which may be quite near the mark, for it would be a long time before anything remotely resembling the conventional image of a thriving Abbey would have risen from the Abbotsbury valley floor. When the first monks went to Fountains in Yorkshire, their only shelter was a leafy canopy round the trunk of an elm tree, and when Orc and Tola summoned the little group of Benedictines from Cerne, they probably fared little better.

But times were changing. It wasn't just the "white mantle" of new buildings that followed the Norman invasion, it was a complete cultural shift that is still around if you know where to look. One example, and not an original one ~ we have different words for farm animals when they are still on the farm (cow, sheep, pig) from when they arrive in the kitchen (beef, mutton, pork). The former are of Saxon origin, and the latter are French terms. Why ? Because, say the linguists, the Saxons were the farm labourers, and the Normans only encountered their products when they were served at table. A small thing, but an indication of how deeply the cultural shift from a Saxon society to a Norman one bit in to everyday life.

The new community in Abbotsbury virtually coincided with the arrival of Norman ways, and the monks would have been organised after the manner of Benedictine houses all over Europe. Supporting the Abbot's gentle care (for, according to the Benedictine Rule, he *"ought to be of help rather than to command ... lest, while he is too desirous of removing the rust, the vessel be broken"*) would have been a Prior, a Precentor and a Sacrist, a Cellarer, Kitchener, Fraterer and Chamberlain, a Master of the Farmery, Hosteller and Almoner, and not at all least, a Bailiff. Why were there quite so many officers ? Did that collection leave any other ranks at all ? Well, remember that all monks were part-time workers: everyone in the community met in the Abbey church seven times a day for prayer.

Each day began at first light with Lauds, and continued thus with prayer at three-hourly intervals, until Compline ended the sequence at dusk. The monk's waking hours were therefore divided into equal periods of work, worship, study and rest ~ apart from Sundays, which were given over to reading (or for the weak or illiterate, to appropriate light duties), and harvest, when it was all hands to the fields.

From a modern, functional, performance-management viewpoint, this is a grossly inefficient way to run what would have been a substantial business, but the monastic view was different. "Orare est laborare, laborare est orare", (to pray is to work, to work is to pray) ran an early monastic saying. And, prayers aside, our Abbey *was* a business, and all those officers were necessary.

> *"A monastery should, if possible, be so arranged that everything necessary - that is, water, a mill, a garden, a bakery - may be available, and different trades be carried on, within the monastery; so that there shall be no need for the monks to wander about outside. For this is not at all good for their souls."*

Keeping order among a group of unworldly and sometimes ill-educated men called for great reserves of diplomacy and integrity, especially in the golden years when covetous Kings cast their eyes over the riches of the great religious houses; for if individual monks owned not even the two sets of clothes they stood up (and slept) in, the community as a whole owned great wealth in both land and kind.

The first staffing requirement, then, was for an *Abbot*, supported by a *Prior* as his deputy, whose roles were to oversee the life and values of the enterprise. The measure of their success is that English culture survived as well as it did, and the measure of their failure is that the origins of English education don't lie more than they do in the monastic foundations which held the only libraries and teaching facilities in their localities.

But the real heart of any monastic community was the worship in its Abbey church, which in Abbotsbury's case was fully three times the size of the parish church. This worship was seemly and dignified (none of your happy-clappy exuberance, thank you very much), and expressed in the Gregorian chant which still sells CDs today. The *Precentor* taught the novices how to sing, organised the Abbey music, and kept the Abbey library: a major responsibility in the days when, if you wanted a new book, it had to be written for you by hand, and if you were asked to lend a book to another monastery, you demanded its value in cash as a deposit on the loan. The *Sacrist* did everything else that the church required ~ kept the building clean, provided the candles for lighting and ceremonial, looked after the vessels for Mass, set out the vestments, and organised everything that a modern verger does, except turn up the heating, for the only Abbey building to enjoy a fire in winter was the infirmary.

Monks took vows for life, so the elderly, senile, infirm and dying were in the care of the more able brothers; hence the the *Master of the Farmery*, working with the *Cellarer*, who not only organised the provision of food and drink, but had a hand in the business of getting it in from the fields, orchards, mills and farms that all belonged to the Abbey. Meanwhile, the *Kitchener* looked after the fabric of kitchens capable of catering on a commercial scale, and it's hardly surprising that the duties of the dining room ~ tables, cutlery, crockery and cleaning ~ fell to yet another officer, the *Fraterer*, who also tended to the sophisticated lavatory system, while the *Chamberlain* cared for all the domestic chambers ("chambres", another word imported from Normandy) in the Abbey.

Mediæval Abbeys were the Travelodges of their day, with the significant difference that nobody was obliged to pay, least of all the great and the good on their various expeditions around the country. The monk responsible for hospitality was the *Hosteller*, and a tough time he must have had of it, dealing at one moment with aggressive beggars, and at the next with guests who might hold the fate of the Abbey in their hands.

That leaves only two officers to make up the complement ~ the *Almoner*, who organised charitable services to the community, and the *Bailiff*, who collected the rents and kept the Abbey accounts. The monasteries may not have had as good a record on the educational or charity front as they should have had, but they were as keen as any other landlord in getting the most out of their substantial farms.

Routine was all; the daily cycle of psalm and prayer, work and rest, the parallel yearly cycles of seed time and harvest, Advent, Christmas, Easter and Pentecost, and the longer rhythm of the centuries.

~~~~~~~~~~~~~~~~~~~~~~~~~~~~~~~~~

For three and half centuries, life went peaceably on, until things came to a sudden and horrific halt when a ship sailed into Weymouth in the late summer of 1348 with a deadly cargo on board. Within a year, *"the boils, abscesses and pustules which erupted on the legs and in the armpits"* had felled their victims as far away as Scotland, and the first invasion of what men called the Black Death had killed a third of Europe. It was inevitable that Abbotsbury would be one of the first places to succumb: the Abbot was dead before Christmas.

It was never easy to find men competent to manage monasteries at the best of times, and it must have been immeasurably harder when the pool of available talent had been drained all but dry by the fatal epidemic. Little wonder, then, that the Abbot elected in 1349 was such a thundering disaster. His name was Walter de Stokes and in four tumultuous years he and his cronies crippled the Abbey.

Quite early on, somebody complained to the Bishop of Salisbury, who inspected the Abbey and tried to pull the house into line without success. Eventually, the Bishop summoned the Abbot and his staff to Salisbury to explain why his orders had been ignored. Unfortunately, his Grace was engaged elsewhere on the due date, and the episcopal rocket was delivered by a team of deputies. It didn't make a blind bit of difference, and the Abbey continued to run up its debts. By the time the unauthorised overdraft had topped £500 (perhaps around £265,000 today), the King had called in the receivers, and the Abbot clearly had to go.

That's when the real fighting began. The bailiffs ordered the Abbot off the premises until the debts could be cleared; they cut off his perks which included comfortable accommodation inside the Abbey walls, personal servants, a food and clothing allowance, and a team of horses. This put him into a monumental sulk. He stayed put, refused to take part in Abbey life and work, but still managed to complain to the Archbishop of York (who, poor soul, had nothing to do with the whole messy business) that he was being compelled to go out and about on Abbey business half-naked and on foot with great holes in his shoes. The fact that he had been forbidden to take any part in Abbey business at all didn't seem to cross his mind.

The rest of the Abbey community struggled on, despite the efforts of the Abbot to disrupt everything they did. He, or one of his cabal, made off with the Abbey seal, a critical ploy, for the seal authenticated legal documents more fully than a signature which could be forged. The seal was put to regular use in dodgy land deals by which the Abbot funded his lifestyle and added to the Abbey debts, nearly doubling them to over £850 (well over £450,000 today) by the time he finally died, in 1354.

Ironically, it might have been Abbot Walter's reckless extravagance and dissolution which inadvertently led to the golden age of Abbotsbury Abbey, for the community acquired or renewed its patronage of several parishes, which helped to build up the income of the house. That, and the more earthly patronage of noble families who chose to purchase their graves in the holy precincts of an Abbey, helped to fund the explosion of building here that began in the last hundred years of the Abbey's life.

But that's jumping ahead a little. Another slippery Abbot was to come out of the mists before then: eighty years on, and another poor Bishop of Salisbury had cause to chastise Abbotsbury. This time, it was wine and women, if not song, that was the cause of it all. The Abbey officers had grown slipshod in drafting the terms of their grants, perhaps because their minds were otherwise preoccupied, if not actually addled. The Bishop advised them gently not to buy more wine than they needed, and to serve it in smaller glasses. That much was in the spirit of the Benedictine Rule, which has it that *"because in our day, it is not possible to persuade the monks of this, let us agree at least to the fact that we should not drink to excess, but sparingly."* Unfortunately, the wine consumption had led, it seems, to other, darker, matters, and one can only guess why the Bishop prohibited the admission of women to the Abbey, threatened the Abbot with suspension if any two people spotted him breaking the ban, and forbade the monks as a body to "resort to a certain chamber for the purpose of *confabulation.*" This time, release from the trouble came about through the resignation, not the death, of the Abbot. Perhaps the ban was too much for him. Or the wine was too sparing.

We shouldn't be too hard on the brothers of Abbotsbury. Three lapses from grace recorded in 500 years; one of them in the aftershock of the Black Death (and who knows how any of us would behave if a third of our neighbours had died of the same infectious disease inside six months ?), the one just described, and one ~ still to come ~ which might have been no more than over-zealous asset management shopped by a jealous whistle-blower. Our monks were no better and no worse than their fellows elsewhere.

In July, 1998, a team of archaeologists published what they had learned from the skeletons of monks buried in East London in the 12th to 14th centuries.   Many of them (the monks, not the scientists) suffered from what the report called "an occupational disease of the higher clergy" ~ diffuse idiopathic skeletal hyperostosis, a condition associated with too rich a diet   The skeletons suffered from none of the "dietary deficiencies commonly seen in lay cemeteries." In other words, they ate like pigs.

That was not what St Benedict had in mind when he gathered the first little group of pious men who would follow the rules of life he had laid out 500 years before the Benedictine community came to the Abbotsbury valley. *"Let two dishes suffice for the brethren: or if fruits or fresh vegetables are obtainable, a third may be added. .... But if unusually heavy work has been done it shall be in the discretion and power of the abbot to make some addition; avoiding excess, above all things, that no monk be overtaken by indigestion. .... All must abstain from the flesh of four-footed beasts, except the delicate and the sick."*   (That, incidentally, was what rather changed the prospects of the swans that dwelt on the Fleet.)

The real miracle of the monastic life is that these men, for all their lapses, contrived to put up such magnificent memorials to the faith from which they so often slipped ~ *"the Abbotsbury fathers reared up stately seemly building after building, of mellow ochry ashlar, to glow in the evening suns of half a millennium"*, once wrote HJ Moule.   Tragically, only a fragment of what they reared up is left standing, but enough is left for today's visitors to guess at the rest, if they only use their eyes and their imagination.

Close to the seaward side of the parish church, look between the gravestones, and you'll see the strip of low wall which is all that remains of the once great Abbey church.   Between the church and the slope that falls away to the pond and the Tithe Barn, stood most of the Abbey's accommodation, the quadrangle with the living quarters above and behind the cloisters where much of the daily work went on.

But the most important area of the Abbey lay at the eastern end of its great church.   Here were the chantries and chapels erected in response to a belief as logical as it is mediæval.   If, when you die, your soul has to be made fit for the after-life, and if the celebration of a Mass to that end is an effective way of reaching that happy state, then putting up the money to build a richly-housed altar where a priest (salaried from the same money) can celebrate Mass in perpetuity, has to be a sound investment.

In the event, none of those piously-endowed chapels lasted for more than a century, a sorry end to the buildings *"of the most excellent workmanship"* (Gerard again) and to all the arrangements for yearly (and sometimes daily) Mass; an end to the purchase of wax candles for the altar and the choir stalls, an end to the gifts of bread for the poor of the parish on the anniversaries of the benefactors' deaths, an end to the payments for the tolling of the bells and the proclamation of the Mass, an end even to the payment to a poor man, selected by the Abbot, to be present to share in the celebration.   All gone, the chapels of St Mary, St Andrew and St Anne, the Clopton chantry and the Strangways chantry, and with them all the tombs of the landed gentry who, according to Gerard *"soe dearlie bought their sepulchres, they have not now soe much priviledge as those that bee in open church yards."*   But we're running ahead of ourselves.   Back to the mind's-eye tour of the one-time Abbey.

All that remains on that empty plateau, once filled with buildings and activity, is one lonely gable wall.   This is the "Pynion end", a strange term until you learn that "pignon" is what French builders still call a gable, and it marks that boundary of the main Abbey complex, for the ground beyond is too steep for building work.   In other directions, the Abbey spread further: towards today's car park lay the Abbot's lodgings, parts of which are still visible around the later Abbey House; and beyond them, one of several mills that the Abbey owned and managed, while on the lower ground towards the sea you can still see one of the fishponds that allowed the monks to eat hugely while keeping the spirit of the Benedictine rule.

And behind the pond stood the Tithe Barn.   Stood ?   It's still there, isn't it ?   Not quite; what's left is only half of the original, and what is now a hollow courtyard on the left of the present Barn was the other half, with a second great arched door through which trundled the carts with the grain from the Abbey's own farms and the farmers who reluctantly paid their dues of one tenth (a "tithe") of their annual harvest to the Abbey.   *We've cheated the parson, we'll cheat him again, for why should the vicar have one in ten ?"* ran the harvest chorus.   Behind and beyond the Barn still stands the dovecote (another source of two-legged protein), and over to the right, across the road to the Swannery (also part of the Abbey larder), were acres of market garden.

This is not, of course, the way the mediæval visitor would have approached the Abbey.   Such would have entered by the gatehouse that once straddled the road that now leads from the village to the Tithe Barn. All that remains of the gatehouse are the bases of its arched entrance, but here you would have passed into the care of the guestmaster, who would have escorted you round to the left and in to the quadrangle ~ not through the archway to Abbey House, which is a much later entrance.   If you had come from the other direction, you would have entered by another gatehouse, now a handsome private dwelling as you drop down the hill towards today's children's farm.   What the Abbots and monks would have made of the tourist attractions that have sprung up in what was once their grain store is anybody's guess.

One building, though, symbolises Abbotsbury so much that it rivals the ubiquitous swan as the image which sells the village today. On top of its terraced hill stands the Chapel of St Catherine, dedicated because of its site to the lady who unwittingly gave her name to a firework by virtue of having been done to death on a wheel.

According to the legend (and it's no more than that, like all the best stories), Catherine was a 4th century girl of Alexandria who defended her Christian faith in the face of argument with philosophers, and then a proposal of marriage, followed by torture, both equally forcefully offered by the Roman Emperor of the day. The embroidery of the tale mounted over the centuries ~ her body, it was claimed, was transported by angels to Mount Sinai, where her relics are enshrined in the monastery that bears her name and to which rich tourists are today transported by the thousand on package tours. Her memory is still celebrated every year on 25 November by a service in the Chapel, to which ought to come every nurse, philosopher, priest, student, wheelwright, miller, spinner, and above all spinster in the village, for she is the patron saint of them all. If hills have patron saints, look no further than St Catherine; there are at least four hills in Dorset with a Catherine connection, for she is patron saint, believe me if you will, of hills.   But it is the spinster connection that is most quoted about our Chapel, and the belief that prayer can work miracles ....

Sweet St Catherine send me a husband.
A good one I pray.
But arn-a-one better than narn-a-one
Oh St Catherine, lend me thine aid,
And grant that I never may die an old maid.

Apart from the fact that it scans better, this version lacks the air of desperation of the one which lays down the requirements for the ideal husband and ends with the words "and soon, St Catherine."   Even the saintliest among us dislike being ordered around, but the prayer itself has a sound reputation, and I have heard accounts of level-headed American ladies crossing the Atlantic on the ancient mission on the recommendation of equally sane friends, and the Chapel is a magical place, whether it be on winter mornings when it hovers in the mists or summer evenings when the "Chapel rings" (be they strip lynchets, relics of the Abbey vineyards, or the vestiges of a pilgrims' way) are sharply highlighted by the setting sun.

The end of the Abbey was achieved with duplicitous formality.   Even if the glory days of the monasteries had long gone, and the 800 houses left had only a handful of monks or nuns each within their walls, it would still have caused a stir if the monasteries were simply handed over to the King who so badly needed the money and the land.   Between them these little groups of men and women owned between 20% and 30% of English soil: the process of parting the monks from their money had to be handled stealthily and diplomatically.

Step one was to put an Act of Supremacy through Parliament in 1534: from then on, any priest, Abbot or Bishop who ventured to question what the King was up to with the Church was by definition guilty of treason.

25

Step two was a law that the taxes paid to Rome by the monasteries should henceforth go to the Crown. Somebody therefore had to assess just how much money that might produce. Within a year, teams of commissioners had pounded the muddy lanes of England from end to end (two of them covered 100 miles and visited 120 houses in the worst two months of 1536) to come up with the answer.

Step three used the reports of the commissioners to justify the "Act of Suppression" which enforced the closure of the smaller religious houses on the grounds of their gross immorality. One of our monks, incidentally, chose that moment to denounce his Abbot. We're back in the realm of shady deals over sales of timber, jewellery, and perhaps the sale of the *Zacharias Chrysopolitanus*, the removal of important legal papers, dealings (presumably under the counter) with the commissioners for the dissolution, and inevitably with a breach of the poor Bishop of Salisbury's fruitless ban on women in the precincts. This Abbot, if his disaffected brother is to be believed, *"hath an abominable rule wyth kepying of wymen, nott wyth i,ii, or iii, but wyth manie more than I doe wryte off":* no wonder that the last Abbot of Abbotsbury, as the complaint went on, had no time for religion, nor for conversation with his fellow monks.

Maybe they were a pretty rotten bunch, and maybe Abbotsbury's Brother Grey was not driven by base motives when he grassed on his Abbot, but the poor frightened men in their cavernous empty house had little room for negotiation when the King's officers bullied them into choosing between promising impossible vows (how could they run their estates if they agreed to be confined to their houses at all times ?), moving to a larger house (which might itself come quickly under threat of closure), or accepting a reasonable pension. It was the pension that sealed their fate: having taken the King's shilling, what chance was there of any of them protesting at the pitiless suppression of *"a rhythm that had endured for centuries and that had been familiar to Englishmen from the very dawn of national history."*

"Duplicitous formality" ? Formality there was, and plenty of it, with the valuations being carefully recorded, the debts honoured, the pensions paid, and places found as parish priests; but nonetheless, duplicity lay behind the whole affair. Before the first of the commissioners had set off, or the 1534 Act had been proclaimed, a letter to Erasmus in Rotterdam reported that the King had said he would *"hand over the monasteries to his barons, so that when they have demolished them, they could use them as they wished."* And, as soon as the rumour of closure began, *"the air was thick with wings making for the carrion"* That's not me being spiteful, it's the author of the standard history of the Religious Orders in England, and if he sounds a little harsh, a Victorian historian comments that *"while the great revolution which struck down the Church was in progress, England simply held her breath. It is only through the stray depositions of Royal spies that we catch a glimpse of the wrath and hate which lay seething under this terrible silence of a whole people. For the silence was a silence of terror."*

It was in such a silence that Sir Giles Strangways came to Abbotsbury.

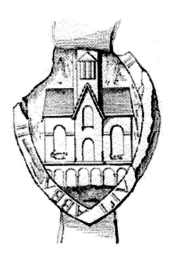

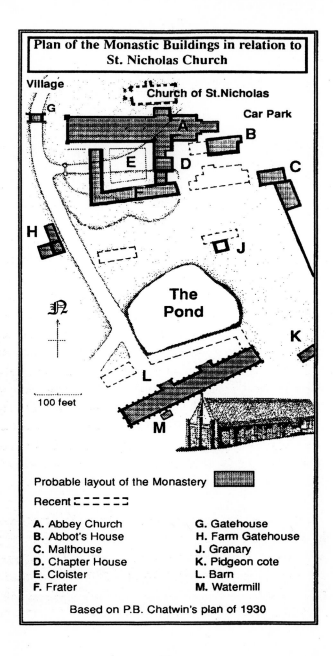

Plan of the Monastic Buildings in relation to St. Nicholas Church

Village

Church of St.Nicholas

Car Park

G

A

B

E

D

C

H

J

The Pond

K

100 feet

L

M

Probable layout of the Monastery

Recent

A. Abbey Church
B. Abbot's House
C. Malthouse
D. Chapter House
E. Cloister
F. Frater

G. Gatehouse
H. Farm Gatehouse
J. Granary
K. Pidgeon cote
L. Barn
M. Watermill

Based on P.B. Chatwin's plan of 1930

Four

Another King, another man

"Strangeways Hall," mused a visitor in the village square, "I wonder if that's got any connection with Strangeways prison in Manchester ?" He might have a point. The family came from up north quite a few hundred years ago, long before they came to Dorset, or on to Abbotsbury.

But before we come to the beginnings of the Strangways, we need to turn to the end of the Abbey. There must have been a dramatic falling away of fortune in its final fifty years: at the turn of the 1500s, the great buildings were still comparatively new, and the richly endowed chapels and chantries spoke of Abbotsbury Abbey's continuing religious influence. But by 1539, when the commissioners came to pension off the monks and claim their estates for the Crown, only eight people remained inside the Abbey walls. The historians who argue that the monasteries had outlived their usefulness have a point, but it still can't have been easy for those eight men to have faced a totally new way of life with only a niggardly pension to smooth their passing. The last Abbot was the exception, being paid off more generously and being smoothly installed as the vicar of the parish. The lesser brethren went off into the unknown with only £5 or £6 in their pockets ~ even Brother Grey, who shopped his superior.

Trying to unscramble what led up to the day when the doors were locked behind the departing brothers is a task worthy of fraud enquiry skills. Brother Gray may not have been wholly malicious in his complaints; any intelligent Abbot in the 1530s busied himself with the wholesale disposal of land and the settling of monastic contracts in such a way that the Crown would have to foot the bill when the long-heralded change-over took place.

Both the ploys ~ the land sales and the legal snares ~ were spotted and set aside by the teams of lawyers and civil servants who carried the dissolution process through and who, like Jack Horner (whose plum was the Abbey of Mells and of whom we shall hear more later), sometimes saw to it that some of the proceeds of the process came their way. This was not just a matter of greed, it was sound domestic policy: the wider the handout of monastic land, the lower the chances of protest at the wholesale disruption of religious life, especially as the transfer of monastic buildings implied selling off assets like the lead on the roofs of redundant Abbey churches, or in our case including a clause to enforce the wholesale destruction of everything inside the Abbey grounds. As a member of a family with a significant stake in Abbotsbury and its Abbey (remember the chantry that was built only 34 years before), Sir Giles Strangways was a prime candidate for consideration in the calculations of local politics, if trouble with the local people was to be minimised.

The politics of owning land have always played a large part in English social and economic life. To my mind, it's significant that Sir Giles initially held his new estate only on a 20-year lease ~ Henry VIII reaped £100,000 (nearly £35 million in today's money) across the country from selling off the monasteries, but the sales came on terms which allowed him to hold the threat of cancelling leases over any new landowner whose loyalty turned dubious. Only later, when the King needed more money for his French adventures, were leases turned into freeholds, and another £800,000 added to the Royal wallet, £1,906 10s of which came from the sale of the Abbotsbury freehold. If the deed were done today, the Treasury would have collected over £275 million, of which over £650,000 would be Abbotsbury's share.

All very neatly done, except for one angle the King might not have anticipated: by creating a whole new class of wealthy landowners, the King had established an alliance of interest that would one day prove fatal to his descendants. Sir Giles, then, got more out of the deal than the King: his Abbotsbury purchase merely added to his already significant holdings in Dorset. As I mentioned just now, Sir Giles was not the first of his name to feature in Dorset history.

The family seems now to have always been there on the edge of great events ~ never quite at the heart of things (though Sir Giles was apparently on duty for Dorset at the Field of the Cloth of Gold), but generally being quietly useful; a safe pair of hands in the view of more than one monarch.

But they were not Dorset folk in the beginning, they were Northerners, with branches of the family strategically placed in both the Yorkist and Lancastrian camps (hence the "Strangeways" reference not being a complete misconception), and it was from Yorkshire that a stepson of Edward IV brought the family down to Dorset in the 15th century. Within fifty years of their arrival, Thomas Strangways commissioned the Abbotsbury chantry, and inside their first hundred years down south, the family owned the former Abbey and all its land. They still do.

~~~~~~~~~~~~~~~~~~~~~~~~~~~~~~~~~~~

Sir John Strangways, son of the Sir Giles who bought our village, was unlucky enough to be Sheriff of Dorset when Good Queen Bess ordered Henry Howard of Bindon to hand over the wife he was in the habit of beating up. He had to stand by when Howard, in response to the royal request, "lifted his leg and let fly behind", which Sir John delicately suggested might be a comment on the court. The safe pair of hands, again, for the same Sir John was one of three men charged with mustering the Dorset contingent against the threat of an Armada landing in 1588.

Forty or fifty years on, and the Strangways family were in the thick of the Civil War. That's not the simple statement it seems to be. The war had its roots in simmering quarrels that had been going on ever since the Scots King James VI & I had ridden south to London and failed to grasp that the English clergy and gentry were not cast in the same mould as the chiefs of his Scots clans or the Fathers of the Kirk. Twenty years before the war flared up in earnest, Sir John Strangways was manipulating elections by the simple device of locking the opposition out of the polling station until his man had enough votes, and a year later he was in prison for resisting King Charles' arbitrary taxation regime. His son married the sister of one of the men who signed the King's death warrant, yet this is the man who risked all to hold Abbotsbury for the same King, while the man who led the Parliamentary troops against the Strangways garrison had himself changed sides only months before, and would change back again in due course. Such is the way of civil war.

Sir John Strangways was loyal to his King ~ a costly stand as it turned out, but risky from the outset, because one of the first things Charles I did when he inherited his Scottish kingdom, was to reclaim all former Church lands that had passed into lay ownership. If he had managed to pull off that trick south of the border, Abbotsbury might have been a very different place indeed. On the other hand, the King would have so enraged the landed gentry that he might still have lost his head, without the prior inconvenience of a Civil War.

Fantasising aside, Abbotsbury was a strategic spot, because it stood on the western route from Weymouth, the nearest point to France on the south coast, other than Kent. If Portland could be held for the Crown, foreign troops could link up with Royalist garrisons at Exeter or Oxford; but with Abbotsbury in Parliamentary hands, the link with the sea would be blocked. The Strangways family were determined to keep that link open.

The story of the siege is well known in Dorset. It's said that history is always written by the victor, and Sir Anthony Ashley Cooper filed his report as soon as the dust and ashes had settled. They came over the hill from Dorchester, a whole brigade of them, ten regiments in all, in an October dusk, and if they set to at once, the fight must have gone into the middle of the night. Perhaps each side gave the other the honour the luxury of a last night's sleep. The siege opened chivalrously enough on both sides: a formal call to surrender and the defiant reply of a "bloody flag" hung out of a window. Then, as now, the parish church stood between the great house on the Abbey site and the village, and acted as a first line of defence, held by a dozen or so men who were quickly taken, but not before the pulpit was wounded in the crossfire.

From then on, it must have been a foregone conclusion. On the Strangways side, a grim determination to hold the pass at all costs against hopeless odds, and on the other, the equally grim decision to make an example of this troublesome band, and send out a warning to others who might get in the way. First, the gatehouse was put to flames, then the hall porch, while the musket fire rained so hard that the trapped Royalists dared not show a face at any window. While all that went on at the front of the house, the heavier guns pounded the back. Only when the whole house was blazing was there any sign of weakness from inside, and when a plea for mercy did come it was turned down *pour encourager les autres*. That's when it all became a typically military mess.

Out front, the top man was digging in his heels, unaware that round the back some of his officers were being a little more generous. Misplaced chivalry; for having given quarter, the besiegers poured in to the house by the back door to pick up whatever they could carry. No matter that the whole place was an ammunition store for the area, or that the flames were lighting up the sky..... The outcome was all too predictable, and eighty looters were flung out a lot more quickly than they had swarmed in. At the end of it all, the score was 75 dead, but it was still the side with the highest body count that won the day. The house was a wreck and was never rebuilt, though bits of it crop up all round the village to this day. Ashley Cooper, having changed sides from King to Parliament, changed back again when Cromwell died, negotiated the return of the King and was rewarded by becoming Lord Shaftesbury: one of his descendants is commemorated in Piccadilly Circus.

The Civil War left other scars on the Strangways family. Colonel James was taken prisoner after the siege, while Sir John and his son Giles went to the Tower. Even on his release, Sir John was held under virtual house arrest at Melbury, and used some of his time to write out a 250-line mental journey in verse around his estates in Dorset, Somerset and Devon, and among the Dorset ones ~

> *"..... along by the sea syde*
> *To Abbotsbury I did ryde*
> *Where all the dwellers in that town*
> *Me only for their landlord owne.*
> *The parsonage, Mills and Demayne lands*
> *Pay all their profitts to my hands.*
> *And here before I farther go*
> *I think it fitt to let you know*
> *Though I that parsonage hold in fee*
> *That right by purchase came to me."*

If the note is defensive in places, it was prudent of Sir John to stake his claim so clearly. His estate had been sequestered, a lawyer's way of saying that two-thirds of his income had been confiscated by Parliament. Lady Grace, as sturdy a fighter as her husband, demanded some of it back, not least because the people who had seized the family estate were quartering their troops on it, and to her credit, she won her case.

The war eventually ended, after the Commonwealth aberration, and the King's son was back on the throne by 1660, thanks in part to the £100 ~ or was it £300 ? (anyway, somewhere between £8,000 and £24,000 today) that Sir Giles gave him to help his escape ten years before, and the family squared the circle by declaring their loyalty to Parliament on the restoration of the Monarchy. A costly venture, for the fines paid by Sir Giles and his family have been estimated at £35,000, a cool £2.75 million in today's terms.

A century and a half beyond these grim days, and things became really quite complicated when our Dorset family joined the high life of London.

Down here in Dorset, the family were now calling themselves Strangways-Horner because Susannah Strangways had married Thomas Horner of Mells (descendant of the Jack who pulled out the Mells plum at the time Susannah's ancestors had bought Abbotsbury)   In London, the star of the Fox family was rising in the form of the sons of Sir Stephen Fox (who founded the Chelsea Hospital for which Charles II has tended to claim the credit).   The elder son, also a Stephen, married Elizabeth, daughter of the Susannah just mentioned, and when Stephen became the first Earl of Ilchester, Elizabeth   brought the Ilchester title to Abbotsbury.   Thomas Hardy, in "The First Countess of Wessex", fictionalised Elizabeth's arranged marriage at the age of 13 and how *"the little figured frock in which she had been married was carefully preserved, ... a yellowing pathetic testimony to the small count taken of the happiness of an innocent child in the social strategy of those days ..."*   By all accounts, the little frock is still to be seen at Melbury House.

Henry Fox, Sir Stephen's younger son, married Caroline Lennox, the eldest of the Duke of Richmond's daughters, became Lord Holland (of Holland House, Holland Park, and elegant Kensington streets named after Melbury and Abbotsbury) and fathered three children.   The eldest was yet another Stephen, while the youngest was the Charles James Fox who caroused and plotted with the Prince Regent, and loaned his name to those hunting folk who call their prey "Mr Charlie".

These marriages brought the Abbotsbury squirearchy into a new world, chronicled and then lavishly televised as "The Aristocrats", and the change of focus is mirrored in the changes of name, first to Strangways-Horner and then to Fox-Strangways.   The Holland House set sprawled out to extraordinary lengths, and not simply to local gentry like the Digbys of Sherborne or the Acklands of Killerton, or to titles like Lord Porchester or the Earl of Northampton, but to much more exotic connections.   One of the Lennox girls just missed being Queen of England, and another was the mother of Lord Edward Fitzgerald, key figure in the 1798 rising of the United Irishmen and a man with Abbotsbury connections, having apparently had an affair with the wife of the playwright Sheridan, whose family owned land to the north of the village in Victorian times.

Serenely in the thick of it all, Susan Fox-Strangways, daughter of the First Countess, keeps cropping up in the Holland House set as the country cousin who could still show her metropolitan friends and relations a bit of style. She acted as the go-between in the ill-starred affair between Sarah Lennox and the future George III, Ramsey painted her portrait, as did Reynolds in a triple portrait with Sarah Lennox and Charles James Fox. She loved the theatre, adored David Garrick, eloped with an actor, was loyal to her friends and secured a pension in old age for Sarah Lennox from her one-time Royal paramour. Quite a character.

While Miss Susan was riding the social roller-coaster on her trips to London, her mother and grandmother had been just as busy back home in Abbotsbury. Grandmama, Mrs Strangways-Horner, cultivated the village church and school, both of which benefited from her generosity, though whether the ornate 18th century plaster screen in the church is an unalloyed benefit to an otherwise unassuming 16th century church is open to argument. Less controversial is the way she boosted the vicar's salary, funded the village schoolmaster, and left £100 (around £8,500 today) in her will to support the poor of the village, an endowment which was still paying out a century or more later. And more than two centuries on, we all still benefit from the £50 she left in her will for the repair of St Catherine's Chapel.

Mother, the first Countess, was, by contrast, much more "Homes and Gardens": it was she and her husband who built themselves a holiday home just beyond the edge of the village. The site, an escarpment overlooking the bay, gave them the notion of calling the new house Strangways Castle, but the family have never been lucky with their houses here, and this was no exception. The first one blew up; this one burnt down, and burnt for the ignominious reason that somebody wasn't keeping an eye on the laundry as it dried in front of the fire. At least this house had a decent innings, for the fire was not until 1913. The replacement was built by cowboys using beach sand: the salt leeched everywhere and the house had to be blown up in 1934 once all the fittings had been auctioned off. Somewhere around here is a fine "pine staircase with mahogany hand rail" which went for only £6/10/-.

Abbotsbury was, however, never more than a summer retreat from the ancestral seat at Melbury, and the real legacy of the first Countess is not the abandoned site of Strangways Castle, but the gardens across the road which she began as a way of ensuring fresh vegetables for the the family and their guests. That's matter for a chapter on its own; I can only wonder at the succession of Earls who took the idea into wider realms: to the 3rd Earl, who planted the woods that shelter the gardens and thus allowed the 4th Earl to use his diplomatic bags to bring back all manner of exotics, to the 5th Earl who trebled the acreage, and to the daughter and grand-daughter of the 7th Earl who encouraged a succession of head gardeners to bring the gardens back to life today.

What would the past generations of Strangways make of today's village and its place on the tourist trail ? Delighted, no doubt, that the Tudor investment had paid off, that the land was still being successfully worked, the family still in possession, and the village still thriving. What Sir John of the Civil War would make of Crown and Parliament now, though, is another matter. Susannah Strangways Horner would probably be saddened by the closure of her school, but delighted that its building is still, like the church she endowed, central to village life. And what of the Earls of Ilchester and their gardens ? We'll save that for later.

Five

The Puzzles of the Parish Church

The first thing you must do is forget Bertufus and his church built "in the very infancie of Christianity". Whatever may be left of the church which Orc rebuilt in the days before the Conquest lies, if anywhere, in the corner of the churchyard, on your left as you leave for the path by the Pynion End. Somewhere in that area stood the high altar of the Abbey Church, and it would be that church that was built upon Orc's ~ and therefore Bertufus' ~ much earlier foundation. The parish church was built (as the Victorian builders found when they lowered the porch floor) in the Abbey graveyard.

The puzzles in my title are mostly to do with who built what where and when, and what they knocked down when they built it, and they are puzzles because nothing quite lines up the way it should. Come to the church from the car park, and you'll see a blocked-up window that isn't in the middle of the wall. Stand at the front of the church and look back at the tower, and you'll see that that isn't in the middle either. When I tried to make sense of it all by colouring in a plan of the church with a different colour for each period when part of the church was built or rebuilt, I finished up with what looked like a transatlantic tartan, the colours were so jumbled up. In the end, though, I think I made some sense of it. Whether I can pass that sense on, though, is a different matter.

At its simplest, the process seems to go like this. Some time in the 1300s, about the time they built St Catherine's Chapel, the monks put up a little church for the people of the village that had grown up alongside the Abbey grounds. Maybe they did it out of piety, maybe they didn't want Abbey

39

services to be disturbed by country folk who didn't understand the liturgy. Either way, the parish now had its own church. You can picture the size of the original building fairly easily: as you come in from the porch, the part that was that first little church stretched along the north aisle (the area between the arches and the wall on your left) and the nave, as far left as the steps up to the altar, and as far ahead as the other line of arches. About two-thirds the size of the present church, and a simple enough building.

At the start of the new century, around 1400, a tower was added, central to what was then the west wall; it was only the later additions that made it lop-sided. High up on the wall of the tower is set a tiny figure, older even than the tomb of the Abbot that stands in the porch, and almost pagan in appearance, until you learn its symbolism ~ God the father is seated with Christ his son at his knee, and the dove of the Holy Spirit hovering above. The entire Trinity in stone, and it may have come from Orc's building.

Another hundred years on, and the church was lengthened: perhaps that's why the roof of the new part is higher, and more steeply pitched, than the roof of the nave. The new section put another 15 feet on the church, to provide a separate chancel, the area where the floor rises in front of the altar: one suggestion is that when the little church was lengthened, there were *two* east windows, side by side, of which only the larger one is left. I'm not convinced. Look at the corner on the left beyond the organ, or if you are outside, look at the corner nearest to you (and that curious blank window) as you come in from the village car park,: that's the bit added in the 15th century. As to why the window that isn't in the middle of the wall is blanked off ~ well, you'll have to wait a few paragraphs, and a few hundred years.

Then, in the final glow of the old faith, before the Abbey lights went out for ever, the little church became quite a big church. The Abbey building programme was finished, and the monks turned their attention to providing the growing village with a church more suited to its needs. They faced an awkward situation, as the little church was quite close to the walls of the Abbey church, which limited how far they could extend sideways, and their solution ~ or what seems to have been their solution (maybe the money didn't run to a full-scale rebuilding) ~ was a clever one. What had been the south wall, facing you as you enter the porch, was turned into an arcade, a line of arches, and a new wall was built about 10 feet beyond the new arcade.

To have extended outward in the same way on the north side would have produced a squat and almost square interior, so they built an arcade *inside* the church on the north, about 10 feet in from the wall, to match the new one on the south. The result inside was what looked like a conventional church layout, with an arcaded aisle on either side of the nave, and it's only when you look closely outside that you spot that the tower is now off-centre, and so is what would have been the great east window, made to look that way by the new buttress put in at that time to strengthen the wall. Standing in the churchyard, you might also notice that the wall on the north side has high battlements above the roof line, while the wall on the south is plain. And that, with one exception, is how the church stands today.

But what an exception ! The great plaster reredos that hits you in the eye as soon as you come in from the porch: that is why the east window, which would normally be the crowning glory of a village church, is blanked off. No point in leaving glass there if no light can enter. The reredos, a gilded screen announcing the Ten Commandments to all who could read, would have been quite the height of London fashion when it was placed here by Mrs Strangways Horner in 1751, but what the village folk, vicar included, would have made of it, beats me. You only need to skim through "Under the Greenwood Tree" to see the fuss and feathers that flew around a Dorset village when the vicar wanted to replace the gallery singers and their band with a new-fangled organ.

From the 14th century porch to the 18th century screen, hardly a hundred years went past without somebody adding a bit to the church here or there. Mind you, you've got to look hard at times: the only thing that seemed to have happened in the whole of the 17th century was that somebody put a little doorway into the south aisle ~ Sir John Strangways, perhaps, making it simpler for the family to slip in to church on a Sunday morning from the family home on the Abbey site. If it was, he didn't get much use of it, for the lintel over the door is dated 1636, and his home blew up in 1644, after the famous fight which gave the pulpit its bullet-hole scars.

That's about it for the fabric, more or less. Lots of other things were done around the building, but none of them significantly changed the shape the building had reached. A new plaster ceiling for the chancel went up at about the same time as the 17th century door was inserted, and was definitely made to Sir John's orders, for his family connections are celebrated in the coats of arms that adorn it. The Strangways family connection ~ that 1505 chantry apart ~ was at its closest, though, in the days of Susannah Strangways-Horner. Her most obvious legacy is the screen, but the Paul Lamarie flagon and the silver-gilt cups and plates which she bought for the church at the same time, and were newly fashioned at the time, wouldn't have come cheap (Lamarie is a world-famous name among antique silversmiths), even if they were only a counterpoint to make the articles used for the Communion service as up-to-the-minute as the setting, lit as it was by the then equally modern and fashionable candelabra.

The restorers have been at work, as in so many village churches, but we were lucky enough to escape the worst excesses of the 19th century. The gallery and the roof of the nave date from a time just too early for the Victorians, and the 1885 restoration was little more than a tidying-up operation, though that was when the barrel organ in the gallery gave way to a more conventional instrument ~ shades of the Greenwood Tree were no doubt cast at the time. The roofs of the nave and the tower were restored in 1930, and the furniture was once again shifted around in the 1970s.

Of the earlier days one other tiny fragment remains: part of a window in the south aisle which shows, so said the Ven. WS Moule, who wrote the standard, but long out of print, guidebook to the church in 1927, the face of St Catherine among fragments of mediaeval glass "promiscuously arranged". And of later years, one memorial is very nearly anonymous. In a corner at the back of the church, where you really have to go looking for it, there is a fading photograph of a young man in a College gown. Let Mr Moule explain: this is what he wrote in that 1927 guidebook, when memories were presumably still quite fresh ~

"One carpenter's business remains in Rodden Row. Here, in the year 1882, a young lad, Harry Vine Norman, learned his trade, and afterwards practised it in the village. Hearing the missionary call at a meeting in Weymouth he offered himself for foreign service, 'I have nothing but myself to offer. I offer myself.' With the assistance of the late Lord Ilchester and other friends he was trained at the Warminster Missionary College, and took a six months' course in elementary surgery and medicine at Salisbury Infirmary. In the year 1891 he was sent out to N. China as a lay missionary of the Society for the Propagation of the Gospel. Stationed first at Peking, where he received Holy Orders, in 1896 he was sent to open up work in Yung-ch'ing, a small town fifty miles south of Peking. Here his evangelistic work among the Chinese was most successful, and the training as a craftsman gained at Abbotsbury stood him in good stead. Under his direction, and largely with his own hands, two mission churches were built. During the Boxer Rising of 1900 he, with many of his fellow Christians, was martyred, and both his churches were burnt to the ground. The memory of this able and devoted young missionary is worthy to be preserved in Abbotsbury."

43

Unfortunately, memories fade over the years, though a distant relative has affectionately reconstructed Harry Vine Norman's life story in "The Flight of the Crane", and pasted to the back of the photograph is a brown press cutting which speaks for itself ~

THE MURDER OF THE REV. H NORMAN - Mrs Norman has just received a letter from her son who is with the Naval force in China, and has been investigating the circumstances of the death of his brother, the Rev. Harry Norman, who was murdered on June 1st. He has visited Bishop Scott, who is in charge ... (words illegible) ... and has talked with a Chinese lad who appears to have been a protege of Mr Norman, and was with him when the tragedy occurred. The lad has written the following narrative :- "The Boxers coming from Woo Kir Ying come City of Ying Ching and then made big voice say 'Kill I and kill Mr Norman. Know him is coming to the city.' Then he ran to Chance's. Mandarin and Mandarin say 'I want you to stop my officer. You must go out than he come again.' So he met the Boxers. The Boxers say 'You give me money me forgive you.' Mr Norman say 'I have got no money for you.' The Boxers say 'You go lend', and Mr Norman lend 1,200 from Chance's shop to the Boxers and Boxers to get he to Woo Kir Ying. Shopman say, 'You don't kill this man. If you kill him my money fines no man gives me back.' 'Yes all right', says the Boxers and the shopman go back to his shop, and next day morning make Mr Norman kill and his money and the Boxers never forgive him.' PETER TSON"

As the centenary of his martyrdom nears, it would be a fine gesture if we could keep faith with the young man who left Abbotsbury for the opposite side of the world at such cost.

Six

Centuries of Gathering Mists

The village might have seemed to sleep, but it wasn't asleep at all, because life still had to be lived as the Civil War memories faded. All the same, "Portesham out of the world and Abbotsbury round the corner" was a local saying with some point to it. Our ancestors simply went about their business in their own quiet way, with not a lot from outside to bother them, nor a lot from the village to interest the outside world, apart from the occasional (maybe that should be "regular") fires that ran through the thatched cottages. The Weymouth guide written in 1798 tells of five fires in the previous 25 years, notably the one in 1784 which destroyed 21 houses, which must have been nearly a quarter of the village.

The 350 years from the Civil War to the end of this millennium passed like one of those autumn days around here, when the mist off the sea clouds all the view until a flash of sunlight or a breath of wind reveals the chapel on the hill. Just so flickers into view a flash of information now and then ~ the incidents, the descriptions of the village by visitors like Daniel Defoe, novelist, gossip and spy, the tales passed down by local folk, or the rise and fall of village enterprises. There were great events going on outside and there were dramatic events in the village, but only one or two were thought worth noticing by the people who write down in letters or journals what they consider important. The rest is lost in the mist.

One of the odder incidents to come out of the mist is the Squires case. It all began in 1752, with a claim of kidnap against Mary Squires, and it dragged in the Lord Mayor of London and King George II himself before the truth ~ if truth it were ~ came out. A girl called Mary Canning claimed at law that she had been kidnapped by a gipsy band led by Mary

Squires in the Enfield area. Squires produced an alibi of a sort, but couldn't make it stick, and she was sentenced to death.

That's when the Lord Mayor, for reasons that may become clear in a moment, stepped in. He found dozens of witnesses to back up a very curious tale which involved the Squires family (who were heavily into smuggling) in walking to and fro between Litton Cheney and Abbotsbury for a series of New Year's Eve parties, then walking back to London to look after a sick relative. This new version of events, over-precise and contrived as it was (the term "Abbotsbury evidence" gained passing currency as a euphemism for perjury), was presented in petition to the King, put Mary Canning in the dock in place of Mary Squires, and transported her from there to the colonies. It also led to the claim by the writer of the London Journal, who was clearly a sceptic when it came to cast-iron alibis, that *"All the people of Abbotsbury, including the Vicar, are thieves, smugglers and plunderers of wrecks."* That was perhaps the nearest the cautious editor of the Journal could hint without fear of libel, that His Worship the Lord Mayor was (a) sufficiently engaged in smuggling himself to fear incrimination from the vengeful Squires family, and (b) capable of organising a chain of convenient witnesses all the way from Dorset to the capital. It also suggests how well and how widely organised was the smuggling business. At least, that's one explanation.

Drive through the village for the first time, and what immediately strikes you is the unity of the place: all the roofs are thatched (they aren't, but it looks that way), all the little wooden windows match (but some of them are metal framed), all the doors are the same colour (they aren't, but they used to be in the days when the Estate bought its choice of dark blue paint by the tanker-load). It's an impression that takes some killing off, so forceful is the impact. As a general rule, for what it's worth, thatch and wooden windows means 17th century or even older, while slate roofs and metal windows date from the mid-19th century surge of building by the

3rd Earl of Ilchester. As to the doors, the only thing you can say with any confidence is that a brightly coloured door means ... that somebody has painted it.

The other thing you notice at once are the high pavements. One theory is that they were built so that the owners of the cottages could more easily mount their horses or enter their carriages. I'm not sure that's the reason: at the time the cottages were built, few of the locals could afford horses, let alone carriages. Another theory is that a caring community built them so that the village folk would not be splashed by the passing traffic. That one doesn't (pardon the phrase) hold water ~ at the time the cottages were built, vehicles didn't move fast enough to fling up enough muck to justify the the trouble of building pavements nearly two feet above road level.

Here's my theory. The only places where you find the high pavements are on the uphill side of the road, and the reason for them is sheer peasant cunning. In Rodden Row, the ground level at the back of cottages like ours is at least ten feet above the road. If you are going to build a house on ground that slopes that much, you must either dig deep into the hillside, or build up a platform that will finish up well above ground level. There is a compromise, though ~ dig out half the ground you need from the back, and dump it at the front. The high pavements, I believe, mark the fronts of the platforms for cottages built by men who didn't believe in giving themselves any more work than was absolutely necessary.

One thing that led me a chase in researching this book was a passing remark that the great JMW Turner had sketched our Tithe Barn and that the sketch was in the British Museum. It seemed easy to ask the Museum staff to locate it for me: that was when I found out that if anyone was to find the Tithe Barn sketch for me from the "Turner bequest" that had been rehoused in the Tate Gallery, they would have to rummage through 20,000 drawings and watercolours in nearly 300 sketchbooks. I had no idea *when* Turner had been to Abbotsbury, so couldn't guess which sketchbook to suggest, but a skim through the standard guide to his work sugested that he toured the South Coast in 1811, narrowing the hunt down to a mere three possible sketchbooks. As to what the sketch might look like, a book on Turner's methods was not promising: one illustration showed a typical sketch that was little more than a doodle, dashed off in 1811 up on the Somerset coast. Nine years later, the doodle emerged as a finely detailed engraving of Watchet harbour. I began to fear that the Turner sketch might turn out to be a scribble that never made it to the end product.

The staff at the Tate suggested the Witt Library at the Courtauld Institute in London; apparently they have a photo of virtually every picture ever painted, and a cataloguing system which points you in the right direction. Unfortunately, it wasn't the direction I wanted. Turner had a friend called Girtin, who toured with him on sketching trips, and was no mean artist himself. He also liked our Tithe Barn: he did a postcard-sized watercolour of the Barn and the Chapel in 1794, a slightly larger one in 1800, and four even bigger ones which are now in Leeds and Manchester. Depressingly, one of the textbooks on Turner mentioned that Girtin's work was often confused with Turner's.

That was when *Dorset* magazine printed a piece by Stephen Swann on Turner's time in Dorset which opened with the words *"Turner may have first ventured into Dorset in c.1795 - there is a watercolour in the British Museum by him of Abbotsbury Abbey."* It took only seconds before phoning the writer of the article and finding, at last, the reference number for the sketch among those 300 sketchbooks. TS Eliot has a line about the end of all your searching being to come back to where you started. And that's our Barn, by Turner, on the cover.

~~~~~~~~~~~~~~~~~~~~~~~~~~~~~~~~~~~~~~~

Every year on 13 May, the children of the village parade floral garlands through the village before leaving them at the War Memorial in the churchyard. Behind that statement is quite a story: for a start, 13 May is not a date picked at random. Back in 1582, the calendar had grown so far apart from the solar year that Pope Gregory struck off 11 days to bring the two back into line. Most of Europe bit the bullet, but Britain, sceptic to the last, held out until 1752, and even then the loss of the 11 days caused rioting in the streets and children felt deprived of their birthdays.

Abbotsbury folk simply decided to hold their May Day celebrations on the day that would have been May Day if those Londoners hadn't messed things up, and to this day, we celebrate May Day ~ and Garland Day ~ not on the 1st of the month, but the 13th.

Garland Day is literally handed down from generation to generation. The ladies who today make the garlands carried them as children in the days when their mothers made them, and so on back to the days when every fishing boat in the village had its own garland and carried it out to sea to secure the harvest. Back in 1893, when Philip Morris painted the scene (and hung it in the Royal Academy), there were nearly a dozen boats, and thus a dozen garlands. At the end of the day, there was a ceremony at the Strangways Castle, where every boy was given a new pair of boots, and every girl was given, not a new apron, but the materials to make a new apron. Sexism may have ruled, but it must have been an expensive day for the Strangways hosts, as one account talks of 200 children enjoying the feast in the Castle grounds.

49

Garland Day has had one or two close shaves in recent years. The police tried to stop it in 1954 in a fit of self-righteousness about children begging (where are they over Hallowe'en and Guy Fawkes night ?), but it went ahead as planned, and the Chief Constable had to apologise for getting in the way of tradition. It was an even closer-run thing in 1971, when the two ladies who had made the garlands for years felt that they were no longer up to the five hours of hard work involved, and it was only at the last minute (and too late to avoid cancellation of the traditional day off school) when a couple of replacements took the job on and in what I now know to be typical of the village's response to crisis, everyone mucked in and brought flowers from all around to the stand-in garland makers.

As I've said, in those days Garland Day was a holiday from school, and every child in the village was caught up in the procession. Today, it's an early evening event, but it still seems to involve almost every one of the children who are bussed off daily to Portesham School. And the same families are still making the garlands. Long may their fingers stay green.

~~~~~~

Tourism came early to Abbotsbury: very early indeed, when you think that Defoe made it a stopping point in 1724, but more of that elsewhere. Remarkably early, all the same, when you discover that the anonymous author of that 1798 guide featured us, along with Lulworth and "Shirborne" as *"places worthy the ATTENTION of STRANGERS who visit WEYMOUTH"*. But I'm really thinking more of the snippets that you can glean from old Trade Directories. Abbotsbury was mainly a place for fishermen and farmers in the 1871 Directory, but the village supported two bakers, two grocers, a general stores and a tailor. And it seems to have done very nicely by them all: Sir Frederick Treves (the doctor who harboured the Elephant Man but is better known here as the author of an excellent 1906 guide to Dorset) said that we lived in a *"fat, comfortable, well-to-do village ... a pretty village, moreover, clean and trim, filled with delightful houses and cottages ..."* Compare that to what he thought of Cerne Abbas in the same book: *"The place is empty and decaying and strangely silent. ... There are quaint old shops with bow windows, but the windows are empty of everything but a faded red curtain."*

By 1889, just a few years before Treves gave us that free advertisement, a new grocer had developed drapery as a sideline, while Mr Gibbons at the Post Office was selling "fancy stationery" and patent medicines. A Mrs Green had opened a lodging house, while Mr Green (presumably her husband) cut hair for a living. The Swan Inn was still in the middle of Rodden Row, where it had been in 1871, but didn't have long to run there, as it was replaced by the Reading Room (later to become the Abbotsbury Studios) in 1898 after, it is said, a fire which finished off all the thatched cottages on that side of the road, displacing the Swan to its present site. Perhaps the Post Office's fancy stationery included this picture postcard showing Rodden Row as it used to be, which a visitor bought here in 1913, and is now in the collection of local views built up by Dave Stevens.

Across the road from the old Swan Inn and the blacksmith, Samuel Mundy had apparently branched out into working as a wheelwright. Perhaps he thought he ought to advertise in more detail, as he had previously called himself simply a cooper back in 1871, but a rival wheelwright had by now opened up in the village. Maybe it was because Mr Stoodley was no longer in business, having died in 1889. The Mundy family were at work here until the 1940s, making wheels and barrels, training apprentices, and making and repairing coaches and wagons proudly enough to pose for the photographer outside the doorway which now carries a window engraved with a life-size image of old Samuel himself.

Like many others in the carpentry trade, the business doubled up as the village undertaker, but we don't dwell on the fact that where we now make our cakes and scones, our predecessors made coffins, and occasionally laid them out (sometimes, as you might say, loaded) in our dining room. People have to be down to earth about these things: when an old chap in Portesham died and a messenger cycled over to fetch Mr Mundy from Rodden Row to measure up, the widow was left with only the one bed in the house for that night. A neighbour asked her where she had slept: "In bed with my dead husband. I wasn't afraid of the old b-----d when he was alive; I'm not afraid as he's dead!"

I was once told a tale, by one elderly lady, of another, who had pre-paid her funeral, specifying the white silk coffin lining that was traditional for spinsters (married women were accorded purple): after a short holiday in Paris, the somewhat sheepish lady felt obliged to change the specification of the lining to the palest mauve.... But as I say, I was told it as a tale, and I'm sure it never happened to an Abbotsbury lady.

As the new century opened, the first two tea rooms had opened in the village: at least, I assume that the rival "refreshment rooms" run by Miss Crichell and Mr Gill were not full-scale restaurants. For the more substantial meal, the gentry patronised the Ilchester Hotel, to the extent that one of the rooms above the "public coffee room opening by glass doors on to a lawn" was named the Royal Room after a visit by sundry HRHs and a German HSH, all of which was lovingly set out in the little guidebook, the first for the village, penned by landlord Tom Cooper.

For the lower orders, Mrs Green of the lodging house was now offering apartments, though any similarity to the modern self-catering exercise was likely to be very slight indeed. Tourism in those sunny Edwardian days was a splendidly casual affair. The Estate's Head Gardener, or the Swanherd, would show you round their kingdoms for a small fee which doubtless quenched a thirst later in the day; and as for the Chapel, one pre-1914 guidebook suggests various houses where the key might be found before concluding "anyhow, try the Ilchester Hotel".

On another forty years, but little had changed by the time the 1939 directory was published, though the arrival of "White Geo. motor car propr. Holmleigh" was a sign of things to come. The Post Office was still selling stationery, but so was Mr Ferry (whose mother gave dressmaking lessons to the girls of the village), advertising himself as a "fancy repository & china dealer; agent for Swan postcards", and the two tea rooms (if they were the same two) were being run by Mrs Beale (at the bottom end of Rodden Row) and Mrs Pittman, while Samuel Mundy had handed on the wheelwright's business to his son John.

That much I had collected from trade directories, when the Chesil Magazine (of which more later) reprinted some memories of the village dating back, the editor reckoned, to before 1909 ~

"I will start at Abbotsbury beach coming into Bullers Road. On the left was a fine old Castle. Then you pass the Tropical gardens, then up over Clover lawns to the bottom of Abbotsbury hill. Then into the village. First on the left was the Carpenter's shop owned by old Charlie Hayne. He used to make the Waggons for the farms. Then on the right was the Blacksmith's Shop; he used to do all the Iron work and shoe the horses from the farms.

Next along the road was the Harness maker, old Joe Vivian. Then we pass the bakehouse, baking the bread for the Village. Then came the Barber, old John Green. Then we pass the Grocer's shop run by Mr Burden. Across the square was the dressmaker, Mrs Ferry, and of course the Ilchester Hotel. On the other side of the road was another little shop run by Mr & Mrs Joe Carter. The shoemaker, Mr Gill. On the other side was a little shop run by Mr Richard Dunford, and next the Butcher, Mr Charlie Hodder; he used to kill his own meat. Then on the corner was the Post Office run by Mr and Mrs F Gibbons. Then was the Doctor, Dr Hawkins. Then turning into Rodden Row you come to the Estate Office where you could take all your complaints. The next was the Reading Room and across the road was the Undertaker, old Samuel Mundy. On the top corner was another baker, Mr Charlie Toms and son.

Going up Rosemary Lane on the corner was a market

gardener who sold butter and eggs, old Mr Hurden.
Coming back down Back Street was the House
thatcher and basket maker Old Bill Dunford. That
was 70 years ago when Bill Dunford thatched the
houses. Coming down to the school what a difference
today. Only 2 shops left, and the butcher's, all the
others have gone."

But some of them have come back: the butcher's shop is still here at one
end of the village, and so is a general (and I do mean "general": you can
buy virtually anything there) stores at the other, and a bakery in between
them. The one-time market gardeners may have gone, but their
successors sell their produce on the doorstep; anything from organic
courgettes to sweet peas, gladioli and oil paintings. Mrs Ferry's
dressmaking school may have gone, but you can still have your clothes
altered or mended in the village. The Post Office is still here, though it
has been nomadic of late, but there are tearooms, gift shops and galleries;
and there are precious few services you can't have provided by somebody
in the village, if you only know who to ask. Just as it should be in a
village, but all too rarely is, which is yet another thing which makes
Abbotsbury special.

~~~~~~~~~~~~~~~~~~~~~~~~~~~~

Driving here from Weymouth you might wonder a little about the high
banks on either side of the road by the filling station and again by
Millmead House. They are all that is left of the two railway bridges that
used to cross the road there. Yes, there was once a railway here.

Nearly ten years in the building, and four more before that, while the Earl
of Ilchester dug his influential heels in against the development, the line
was launched in 1885 to help the fishing trade and to ship out the iron ore,
stone, bitumen and, they hinted, the gold that was all claimed to be here for
the working. Tourism also came into the equation, but not in the direction
you might expect. The map with which the promoters sold the line to

investors stressed how easily Abbotsbury could be linked to "the Continental Railways", and there were plans, it is said, to take the line westwards to Penzance, if only the Earl would agree to it crossing his land.

The grand idea was not to be fulfilled that easily, though. In a move reminiscent of the land deals that preceded the dissolution of the Abbey, some shrewd entrepreneurs bought parcels of land along the route of the line, and held out for the highest possible price. The work stopped. New contractors started, not very efficiently. The work stopped again. Then the big boys moved in, and the line finally opened for business with the clout of God's Wonderful Railway behind it. A mile a year in the building, and at the cost of two deaths, but it seemed to be popular. In the first three weeks, 2,500 people and five dogs made the trip to or from Broadwey, and the first year's passenger tally came to a satisfying 45,000, but that was down to novelty and enthusiasm. The figures for both passengers and freight soon began to drop, and the GWR was left with something of a lame duck when it took over control of the line in 1896.

The wonder was that it lasted so long. The iron and stone workings on which it was intended to depend soon came to an end (though the shale oil side picked up in the 1914-18 war years), and nobody mentioned the gold that had been dangled in front of the speculators. The tourist trade became the main business, along with the goods service for local farmers. And the Royal Family used it now and then. On more normal days, the fish train ran when it was needed, and four regulars went back and forward in each direction. The Edwardian tourists were encouraged to stop "at" Upwey Wishing Well ~ actually a stiff walk away from the famous well, there's nothing new about travel agents' poetic licence. In 1903, you could buy a day return from Birmingham to Weymouth for only 5/6d (27½p), with a 1/- (5p) supplement on to Abbotsbury, and in 1937 you could come here on a 12/6d (62½p) holiday season ticket and bomb around the countryside as often as you liked, stopping at any station to Bournemouth or Yeovil on the "Flying Banana" diesel railcars, but the writing was even then on the wall, with 14 different coach companies competing for charabanc outings to the village and the Swannery. The line fought back, offering 6-berth camper coaches at Abbotsbury station for self-catering breaks in 1935 for £3.00 a week: provided you came here by train, booking at least four return tickets from your home station.

The Abbotsbury station master's house ~ Rose Cottage in Rodden Row ~ is still here, but where the station itself stood there now stands a modern bungalow, sitting privately alongside the one-time track, which is now a footpath to Portesham: turn left after you pass Abbotsbury Glebe and follow your nose. Once past the site of the station, you'll pass the engine shed, used for target practice when the local Home Guard learned how to use petrol bombs in anger.

It was the school business that kept the line going as long as it did, carrying pupils to the junction that linked them to both Dorchester and Weymouth. Meetings in the village and lobbying on all sides failed to secure the line, but at least managed to convince Southern National that it should time its Upwey route to maintain those two important links, at least until memories began to fade. When the final trip was made, in December 1952 and thus long before the Beeching axe, over 100 people joined the children on the early train as it pulled out in appropriately foul weather, adorned with the Parish Council's wreath on the engine. More than 30 years later, Brian Jackson penned a fitting epitaph:

"It was the archetypal Great Western rural branch line. At Portesham, you could leave your boots to be mended, have a haircut and then watch the same man issue you with a railway ticket and see you on the train, whilst at Abbotsbury chickens were kept in the goods shed. It was said by a former railwayman, 'you can get anything you want on the Abbotsbury branch if you have the contacts'. "

The War changed the look of the village: one resident of the time remembers roads round here looking "like the Somme" as the tanks rolled by. The line of "dragon's teeth" tank traps appeared on the beach and the pill boxes defaced the hills in preparation for the unfriendly arrival of the VI Panzer Division, just as the earlier hill fort had been made ready to see off those other Saxons a thousand years or more before. Nissen huts went up by the Pynion end, houses were requisitioned, and the whole area became a "prohibited zone": you needed a pass to travel in or out, and you kept a case packed all the time against instant evacuation.

Thinking of the dragon's teeth, I occasionally hear visiting fishermen complaining of the loss of expensive tackle to underwater tank traps, but one occasion that sticks in the mind more than most was the time when an elderly lady at the next table in our Tea Rooms sat silently listening to the grumblers, then remarked once they had left, "What an odd coincidence. I drove the officer who set those traps so long ago. I didn't think I ought to mention that to those men ..."

There were casualties more serious than fishing tackle back then: the plaque in the church may be correct in giving thanks that nobody from the village was killed in action, but the Estate's head keeper was killed by a landmine on the beach, another villager was shot by a US Army guard at New Barn, and a Hurricane pilot fatally crash-landed in the Fleet lagoon where the boffins later tested the bouncing bomb that proved itself on the Dambusters' raid. As British troops were replaced in the run-up to D-Day by Americans who installed a 4-million gallon fuel store by the Hardy monument, ancient cars and motorcycles were resurrected, and all sorts of weird experiments, from rocket-powered rope ladders to floating landing strips designed like Swiss rolls, were tried out along the coast.

But other changes were afoot, less dramatic but equally influential: electricity arrived, stealthily and underground because the Earl would have no unsightly poles around the village, but sanitation remained basic, and great was the rejoicing when the Estate provided a cottager's family with a new bucket for the necessities.   It would be a full twenty years after the end of the war before the real turn-around began.

~~~~~~

The school outlasted the railway.   It's often said that the three things which keep a village stable and active are the pub, the church and the school ~ not necessarily in that order.   We're lucky: two of the three are still here, and still thriving, but it's been a long time since the Strangways Hall was the school it was built to be.

One of the ironies of the closure is that there are now probably more school-age children in Abbotsbury and Portesham separately than there were in the two villages combined when the closure was enforced back in 1973.   Nonetheless, the Abbotsbury school didn't go down without a fight.   Every adult but one in the village signed a petition, and a PTA was set up to take on the campaign.   The background was complicated.   The policy of the Ilchester Estate had been to amalgamate its farms, and thus reduce the labour needed, in turn reducing the number of young families in Abbotsbury village, while there were developments afoot in Portesham: but only a few years ahead, a development plan began to take shape, which would bring just such families back into the area, to modernised cottages or the new houses scheduled for the Glebe estate.   A few forecasts by the Education Authority might not have gone amiss.

Portesham people were not too upset by the closure: they were going to get a better school.   The County Hall apparatchiks said what they usually say on such occasions: words like "cost-effectiveness" might have been bandied around.   The Headmaster argued that the Abbotsbury building was big enough to house both schools, and when the Education Authority put their proposals to the parents, they voted unanimously against them. When the matter came to the Education Committee, that fact wasn't reported, and when the Western Gazette reported that an Abbotsbury meeting had "reluctantly accepted" the closure plan, the balloon went up.

By the time the matter was on the County Hall agenda, the battle lines had been drawn. The voice of reason and hard cash maintained that paying to bus twenty-plus children to and from Portesham to join the forty children there would cost the ratepayers £8,500 less than keeping both schools open. The Abbotsbury parents argued that the Portesham school had already overflowed into the school house and that there was no safe access for coaches from Abbotsbury. In contrast, the Abbotsbury building could take both groups of children, and, it was said, the site offered room to expand. One councillor ~ there's always one like him ~ argued both ways at once, saying that the Abbotsbury children were unfairly privileged and unfairly disadvantaged at the same time, and the Chief Education Officer blinded logic by implying that the school nearer its pupil capacity should be the chosen site.

And so it was done. Nearly twenty years on, there are 90-odd children in the Portesham School which has had to expand to a second site across a busy road, while the Abbotsbury parents have had to fight a campaign to retain the promised free transport to and from Portesham, more than once making their protest known via TV when the Authority tried to offer the children of the village the choice of walking to school along the racetrack road to Portesham, or along the old railway line to an accompaniment of adders, nettles or muddy potholes according to season. Still, we do have a playgroup and a very busy village hall by way of compensation.

~~~~~~~~~~~~~~~~~~~~~~~~~~~~~~~~~~~~~

Dorset food and drink has many local specialities, each with their own secretive quirks. When our local WI ran a competition for Dorset Apple Cake, there were as many recipes as entries, and at Wheelwrights we remain coy about parting with the recipes for either of the two versions of Apple Cake we offer our customers. When a local baker recently retired, the evening paper reported that he wouldn't pass on the recipe for his Portland Dough Cake even to his own relatives who had taken on the business. And then, there's Blue Vinny.

Tradition says it was made in the spring from surplus milk and was called "the poor man's Stilton" because it had only half the fat content of Stilton and was more crumbly. Commercial production, according to Louis Littman of Ashley Chase Dairies, stopped in 1955, though he claims that dealers were importing second-grade Stilton from up north and passing it off as Blue Vinny for a higher price than good Stilton would fetch. The inevitable court case resulted in a definition that Dorset Blue Vinny must be made in the county from skimmed milk with no more than 15% fat content. In other words, Blue Vinny was good for you: if you could find it. In 1972, Kenneth Allsop *"made enquiries in London; Fortnum's don't stock it; Harrods once did but can no longer get it; Selfridges don't have it. Paxton and Whitfield, in Jermyn Street, obtain some now and then, but know of only two sources."*

Ashley Chase, just over the hill from here, started trying to revive Blue Vinny in 1982, but hit a topical snag in that modern dairies are just too hygienic for a cheese that in the old days could be so ripe *"that its eaters would watch the maggots in it race each other down the dining room table"*. Vinny, after all, is Dorset dialect for mouldy from damp or fungus. After a lot of experimenting, they finally got it right for the West End market. Too right, as it happened. The cheese was so popular that the gourmet shops loaded the price to give themselves a profit margin of a gluttonous 175%, while the supermarkets said that their public was *"not adventurous in trying new foods, and that it was not their function to educate people's palates."* By 1985, the Ashley Chase experiment was over, but the unique taste of Blue Vinny is still available in Abbotsbury, though that doesn't commit me to the legend that it was revived because somebody found an antique leather bucket in which the cheese used to be made and discovered that it still preserved the crucial bacteria needed to recreate the original delicacy.

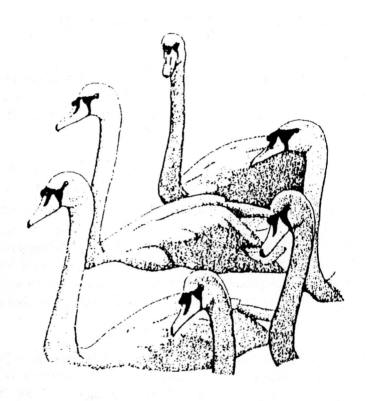

Seven

Beside the Sea Side

THE SWANNERY AND THE FLEET

The Swannery was first recorded in 1393. On the strength of that record, it celebrated its 600th anniversary in 1993, and David Gentleman designed the set of commemorative stamps produced by the Post Office for the occasion.

I don't believe a word of it: the swans were here long before the Abbey. What brought them here was not opportunist monks making the most of the Benedictine Rule which forbids them to eat the meat of four-footed animals, but says nothing about large two-footed birds; no, it was something that was here long before then: it was the eel grass that grows in the shallow waters of the Fleet, and is the basic element in a swan's diet. Poor swans, they just happened to be in the wrong place at the wrong time, but Swanherd Fred Lexster once remarked that the swans knew that they were here long before the Benedictine monks.

The sea may seem calm off Chesil ~ at least it does to one used to North Devon surf, but appearances can deceive. In the morning of 23 November, 1824, a hurricane destroyed the entire village of East Fleet. You might think that being half a mile or so inland might protect you a little from the anger of the sea, but a mast the height of a telegraph pole stands in the Swannery to mark the height of the wave ~ one wave ~ that did just as much damage to the Swannery. According to a boy who watched the storm at Fleet village ...

"Most so soon as twas light a lot of us boys was out where we be a-standing, for to look at the seas what was coming over the ridge. Then after we'd been a-looking a goodish bit a thing happened differ'nt altogether. Twern't a sea - not a bit of it - twer the great sea hisself rose up level like, and come on right over ridge and all, like nothing in this world ... we runned like mad ... till we was nigh up in Chickerell. When we comed back, where was the church ? - all but this firm little chancel - all sucked away by that terrible rise of the sea; went up to that there linchet, he did."

Fleet village was the setting for John Meade Faulkner's "Moonfleet", a classic ripping yarn of smuggling and romance. We sell the paperback in Wheelwrights, and from customers' comments, I've come to the conclusion that I must be the only person in the country who didn't read it at school ~ being a Scot, I was reared on "Treasure Island" instead.

Sorry, I've strayed from the point. Back to the Swannery, which brings me to Dick Dalley, heir to the Lexsters who had been Swanherds here for generations, and now Swanherd himself after 30 years down on the shore of the Fleet. In a profile in the *Daily Telegraph* some time back, he recalled that in his early days he had prepared swans for the table at Melbury House, when there was still an Earl of Ilchester to carry on the monastic gourmet tradition ~ until the last one he sent up the road, which prompted a phone call to the effect that if his Lordship had wanted a bloody sparrow on his dinner table, he could have shot one himself out of the French windows.

Fred Lexster was the third of his family to hold the post of Swanherd: the obituaries in the local press when he died in 1982 told some beguiling tales: badgered by a visitor to sell a swan, Fred (so the paper avers) sold him a pair of gay cobs who made their way back to the Fleet within 24

64

hours. He is reported to have thrown the distinguished ornithologist Erik Hoskins out of the Swannery for disturbing the birds, but he was more charming to the equally distinguished ballerina Anna Pavlova when introduced to her by Thomas Hardy, and prompted her comment "I have now seen the real Swan Lake". Fitting, then, that his funeral cortege was headed by a swan modelled from swan feathers in place of the more conventional wreath.

The idea that swans are vicious birds, ready to lash out at anyone near them is belied by the thousands of visitors who walk through, round, and over the hundreds of cygnets every spring. But even Abbotsbury swans have their weapons to hand and the otherwise amenable birds have broken the odd bone, bent the occasional galvanised bucket, and even killed one large dog, with a blow from their six-foot wings. Any defensive behaviour might be linked to protecting the slow-maturing cygnets. John Fair, a former swanherd, wondered which came first *"the aggressiveness of adults to protect the young, or has the development of the cygnet become slow because the young have adequate protection ?"* The answer might be simpler: as Don Moxom, Warden of the Fleet and Chesil Bank Nature Reserve, pointed out to me, those fluffy little cygnets turn into big birds, and their rate of maturing is no different from any other bird of that size.

This isn't the place to lay out the story of the Swannery in its modern scientific rôle: that is well done in the guide published by the Estate which inherited the Fleet and its "flight of wild swans" from the Abbey. Every so often, though, things crop up which don't make it into the official guidebooks. Things like the gay swan pairs (or even a ménage à trois) have hit the tabloids more than once, offering a fresh angle on the usual sexual gossip column material; or the arrival in 1998 of a larger than usual gang, seven or eight of them, of black swans of no fixed address. Swannery staff checked with Dawlish, the nearest known possibility, but found no absentees. That addition to the colony led to fears of avian racism, eased by the fact that black and white swans breed at different times of year. At least nobody thought of calling them the Magnificent Seven: a few more in the gang, and headlines about the Dirty Dozen would have been irresistible.

Visitors invariably ask if the swans belong to the Queen. The simple answer is that these ones don't, thanks to the Abbey's charters, confirmed to the Strangways family by Elizabeth I, giving today's Estate, like the Dyers and Vintners of Swan-upping fame on the Thames, a Royal licence to own their own "Birds Royal". Good Queen Bess prudently ordered a census of the swans at the time she confirmed the charter: as the price for a brace of swans then ran at 2/6d (about £17 today), perhaps she wanted to be sure that she wasn't doing herself out of a nice little earner.

The history of the Swannery may seem to be a seamless one since the 1393 Swanherd paid the penalty for fiddling with sluice gates on the Fleet, but the numbers have gone up and down quite extensively over the years ~ there were over 1,200 swans here in 1980, but a hundred years before the numbers were dramatically down after heavy storms: one writer claims that all but one of the 1894 crop of cygnets died, but the numbers were back up to 1,200 in Edwardian times. At the biennial round-up in 1999 there were about 600 swans in residence, plus half as many migrants, and biology dictates that there should be around 500 cygnets hatching each spring. In 1996, the Fleet froze over (global warming, the doomsayers said), and our local TV station ran some footage of swans trying to land on the ice with results so humiliating that I, for one, felt embarrassed to be watching the poor birds, who had to be hand-fed for weeks until the cold snap ended. Ironically, in 1998 and again in 1999, the first cygnets arrived well ahead of schedule, and global warming was again blamed for their turning up too early, which seems to be a case of trying to have it both ways at once.

The penalties for harming the birds were always severe, which is how we know that there was a swanherd (and hence a Swannery) in 1393: in 1754, the fine for taking an egg was £5.00 (around £300 today), and the price for killing a swan at the same period was to pay for enough wheat to cover the body of the hung-up swan. Remember that the typical wingspan of a swan is over 6 feet, and you can guess how many sackfuls it would take to meet the fine.

If you notice that the swans seem to swim with one leg cocked up, it doesn't mean that they are crippled, simply that they are keeping that leg warm by lifting it out of the cold water. And ~ another one for Trivial Pursuit ~ our swans ceased to be a "game" when they stopped being kept for food; they are still, however, a "flight" when they are in the air, a "fleet" when they are in the water, and a "herd" because, ever since the Abbey took them over, they have been a managed colony. In short, call them whatever you want, one of the terms is bound to be right some of the time.

And while we're in the "not a lot of people know that" mode, most visitors to the Swannery will have picked up the fact that Abbotsbury swans' feathers have for two centuries been sent regularly to Lloyds of London for use in entering records in the "Doom" Book ~ but how about using the feathers to comb bees out of honey combs because black feathers frighten them ? Or making flutes out of swan wing bones ? OK, they haven't done that since the 11th century, but it's still a curiosity. And if you happen to need a new tobacco pouch, find a spare swan's foot, and use the paddle (that's the skin between the claws) to make one for yourself.

To get around the Fleet you need trows, shallow, punt-like boats that can be sculled or poled in only 4" of water. Made in Edwardian days for the Earl's trigger-happy duck-shooting guests, some of them are still in use today, albeit for less bloodthirsty pursuits, and still regularly repainted in the traditional red and white livery.

Every second year the trows join the little Armada that sets off for the swan round-up, the MOT of the Swannery stock, carried out by a flotilla of boats that slowly surround the swans like the seine-netters of old; only this time the aim is to check every bird for its health ~ and its identity. And a jolly good time is had by all, though nobody seems to ask the swans if they share in the general bonhomie. It can't be too traumatic, though, because as well as the "locals" counted in the 1999 round-up, there were those 300 or more incomers from the Somerset levels while they moulted and waited for the new feathers to grow in. The growing number may be a result of the decline in anglers using lead shot, but the more intriguing question is: how do the young swans who come here for their first annual moulting holiday know about the Swannery ?

Mind you, there are plenty of other birds in on the secret ~ more types of geese than I had ever thought of, Wigeon, Teals and Little Terns (whose nesting arrangements are the subject of some exceptionally high-tech computerised study at the moment) and birds with curious names like Little Stint and Curley Sandpiper which somehow remind me of characters from Dickens or John Buchan.

~~~~~~~~~~~~~~~~~~~~~~~~~~~~~~~

I started this chapter with mention of the great storm of 1824. A storm of a different kind brewed up more recently, when, incredibly, the CEGB tried to slip a nuclear power station on to the landward shore of the Fleet without mentioning the idea to anyone. It was Louis Littman of Ashley Chase who helped to uncover the plot, successfully blew the whistle, then told the story in his account of how he built his "Dorset Domain".

A building the size of a substantial department store, it was scheduled, so the Government spin doctors of the day admitted under pressure, to be placed at Herbury Bay as one of a chain of expensive reactors of the Three Mile Island type "along the south coast", in the teeth of all the evidence that the CEGB had picked the wrong type and had been using suspect figures for their budgetting. More to the local point, Herbury Bay was *not* on the south coast, it was an inlet of the Fleet lagoon and in the very centre of that superb view that opens wide as you crest the hill from

Bridport. It's also the one part of the Fleet that you can see from the road into Weymouth (over to your right just before Bagwell Farm) and, as Littman put it, they *"would have as much chance of getting away with this project as if they had tried to erect their nuclear power station in Kew Gardens."* It pays to be vigilant.

THE SUB-TROPICAL GARDENS

"You can travel the world in these gardens" said Roy Lancaster when he opened the new tearooms there in 1998. Plenty of people did just that in order to put the Gardens there in the first place, though there is an interesting theory that they arrived by accident: having failed to get anything to grow on the slopes closest to the Strangways house by the beach, the gardeners put in a few essentials across the other side of the valley, and found that they thrived. Experimenting with plants a little more exotic led to them being even more adventurous, and the rest, the story goes, is history.

If it *is* history, it is a chequered one: I've met local people who can remember the Gardens many years ago as a neglected wilderness, fallen a long way from the Victorian splendour. But those days have gone, and the splendour is rolling back, year upon year, thanks to the 10-year plan put in place by Head Gardener Stephen Griffiths. The site has a head start owing to the cradling of the hills and the high sweep of oaks around it, while the sea keeps the temperature from too many extremes.

"Rolling back, year upon year" may be more true of recent years than before. Roy Lancaster was complimentary enough in 1998, but he could still write earlier of "the unmistakable air of decline" when he visited the Gardens in the 1960s, and the credit for today's displays should go to Lady Teresa Agnew, her daughter Mrs Townshend, and a succession of head gardeners like John Hussey, John Kelly, and our neighbour Reg Trevett, whose advice we at Wheelwrights shamelessly plunder from time to time. *Country Life* may have enthused about the Gardens in 1899, but nearly 60 years of neglect meant a lot of ground clearance had to be done before the programme of new planting could begin. And after the new planting came the high professionalism that has made the Gardens home to the national reference collections of eucalyptus and salvias.

Home, also, to generations of Strangways family dogs, plus one stranger who deserved an honourable grave: an Airedale which went down with his ship (and his master the Captain) off Portland in 1915. When the loyal dog's body was washed up on the beach, it was bought to the Gardens for burial, and its stone is still there, even if it no longer marks its original resting place.

I must confess that my wife and I don't go round the Gardens as much as we should: it's always that way with attractions on your doorstep ~ but we do have quite a few products of the Garden nurseries in our own little corner, including, as a matter of principle, the Stransvaesia (named after the 4th Strangways Earl who brought it to this country in 1828) that the experts have decreed should now be called a Photinia. We've planted grasses that have run riot, and are hoping for fruit some day from the minute fig tree cuttings we were given this spring and the vines we have planted from local stock. Meanwhile the 6" cutting of a climber called "Lord Ilchester's Earl Grey Rose" is now running along our first floor window sills and heading over our porch only a couple of years after we stuck it in a hole in the pavement. You can see how the professionals do so well when we amateurs can get away with so much.

It's partly down to a micro-climate that can have fuchsias flowering in December while Dorchester roads are covered in ice, but can equally have us wrapped in thick fog while Weymouth sizzles. That's one of the nicer parts of the Dorset climate ~ if it's bad in one part, drive ten miles, and things will be completely different. We all benefit from the special

Abbotsbury climate, but nowhere more than the Gardens valley. Mind you, there's more to it than climate; gardens like these call for patience. Abbotsbury's Monterey cypress may be the tallest one north of the equator, but it was only 60cm tall when it was planted in 1899, and a magnolia planted in 1864 didn't produce a flower until 1900. I don't like to dig plants up just because they seem to be stagnating, but I doubt if I would have waited that long for a result. Nor, I am sure, would I have the patience to dead-head no less than 200 varieties of roses.

Every so often the Gardens take a back seat to form a chameleon-like setting for Abbotsbury Music events. I use that word because it seems odd how different specimens seem to come centre stage according to the music on offer that evening. When Garden Opera presented *Cosi fan Tutte* in the styles of an Edwardian cricketing party in 1998 and *The Marriage of Figaro* as a commentary on sleaze-ridden politics in 1999, it was the conservatory and the great native trees that seemed prominent, yet for the Colombian and Flamenco evenings, the more exotic palms came into their own. The programme of Gardens events grows from summer to summer, and the annual Garden Festival has spread to a cross-village competition for the best floral displays in a front garden or a window box. Fifteen years ago, Abbotsbury Gardens had a stand at the Chelsea Flower Show; now the Chelsea judges come to our Garden Festival.

THE BEACH

If you go walking on the beach, take your eyes off the view now and then and look for a holy stone: not a coventionally sacred one, but one with a hole in the middle ~ *"fragments named by our Saxon ancestors Haligstan"*. So says Llewellyn Powys, who adds *"no one of prudence in the county ever passes a stone with a hole through it with indifference, but is careful to preserve such fortunate fragments for the sake of the good luck they bring. "* If you find a big enough one, it might have retired from its one-time work holding down a seine net. The true "Abbotsbury pebble", though, holed or not, has to be brown with green spots. Beware of imitations.

Today it's all rod-and-line stuff off the beach, but as late as the 1950s there were still half a dozen boats at work here during the summer months, though the catches, varying from dozens to thousands, were far short of the days when "one boat would bring in tens of thousands at one haul". In 1791, a bumper harvest brought the price tumbling down from 1d (0.25p) per 100 all the way to 1/- (5p) per 30-cwt wagon, and in July 1894, a catch was recorded of a staggering 100,000 head of mackerel.

We still have one fish trader in the village, scooting around in a little van labelled "The Fish Wife", which has to be a safer way of transporting her wares than the horse bought by an earlier counterpart. The story goes that Old Grace (or Nanny Gibbs, according to which version you find), swapped her trusty donkey for an Army horse belonging to a Dorchester officer who wanted a donkey for his children. All went well until the fishwife's round took her past the Barracks as the bugle sounded the fall-in. The new mount, minus most of his stock-in-trade but unfortunately plus his hysterical new owner, duly fell in on parade in his accustomed manner alongside his former colleagues.

Back on the beach, the boats in the old days would be out at dawn to "shoot the seine". The lerrets, as they were called, were rowed out in a wide circle from the shore, trailing the end of a seine net weighted down with stones at the bottom, yet held afloat with corks at the top, forming a sort of drawstring bag, 500 feet long and 40 feet wide, with a narrow bit at the end, called "the hose", where ~ you hoped ~ the fish would be crammed together in their thousands. These lerrets were of a special design with bows at both ends to let them land more easily.

The steep incline of the beach made for dramatic launches, as the lerret had to be pushed off sharpish right at the proper point of the wave, and ferociously rowed out before the next wave flung it back on to the pebbles.

When the circle was complete, the far end ropes on the net had been thrown ashore, and a member of the crew had rowed back round to check that the net was hanging properly in the water, the wearisome task would then begin of hauling in the net and closing the trap on the fish. I've seen it done for salmon on a much smaller scale on the Torridge in North Devon, but the uncertainty about the size of the catch is the same. Only towards the end can you tell if your haul is going to be in single figures or in thousands: Cyril Toms writes of catching five hundred stone or more, using dip nets to transfer the mackerel from the slithering mass into pots, and then packing the catch, two stone at a time, into boxes for the early train, while the lerret was pulled ashore on its own oars used as rollers. Those 3-4 hours of work would set anyone up for breakfast, net-mending, or maybe a second shot.

But the mackerel were not the only thing to be landed on the Chesil Beach by Abbotsbury. Every book about the village (including this one) quotes that superior Londoner's claim that *"All the people of Abbotsbury,*

73

including the Vicar, are thieves, smugglers and plunderers of wrecks.''
So what ? Daniel Defoe remarked at about the same time that smuggling was *"the reigning commerce from the mouth of the Thames to the Land's End of Cornwall.''* Who were we to stand out from the crowd ?

Smuggling was nothing more than the unfettered operation of the free market. If brandy cost 5/- (25p) a gallon in France and 32/- (£1.60) in England, a merchant venturer could buy in perfectly legitimate stocks across the Channel, pay a captain and crew to transport the stuff, pay a "lander" to bring it ashore and quietly distribute it to the otherwise law-abiding gentry at half the duty-paid price, and still make a generous profit.

The only part of the deal that was missed out was the payment of the same foolish level of British duty that leads people today to overload their transit vans on the Dover-Calais run; and the only reason the trade was so commonplace then, as now, was that the customs service was hopelessly undermanned and underpaid. And don't compare the "brandy for the parson" trade with today's drug-runners.

The quantities involved ~ like the risks and the penalties ~ were staggeringly high. The vessel of choice was the 9-gallon anker barrel: even a half-anker, holding the equivalent of nearly 23 standard bottles, weighed almost half a hundredweight. If you prefer that in new money, think of a barrel holding 17 litres of spirits and weighing over 25 kilos. No wonder they needed pack horses.

When some 18th century Abbotsbury fishermen found "some small barrels" carefully sunk off the Chesil Beach, and hoisted 23 of them into their boats, they were in luck to the tune of very nearly 550 bottles of brandy galore. No wonder Mr Strangways' bailiff took the collection from them (indeed took them from the customs officer who had legally impounded them), claiming the treasure as a perk of the Lord of the Manor. I have to wonder if he had the chutzpah to claim the ancient rights of sac, soc, tol, infangenthief and the rest of them while he carried

74

off the barrels: certainly one of his ancestors took the precaution of checking with the newly-retired Abbot on the precise terms of the beach, fishing and salvage rights he had just purchased from the King.

From there, the situation descended into farce. The customs officers tried to get the barrels back from the bailiff, but the Abbotsbury men, Strangways employees and tenants to a man, "frighted them out of their goods" without a single blow being struck. Desperate measures were called for: the Army was hauled in from Dorchester, and the barrels were duly handed back; but there was more to come. Mr Strangways lodged a complaint with the Secretary of State for War no less, to the effect that soldiers should not have been employed in a local quarrel about the ownership of salvaged goods, and even managed to have a question about the fracas raised in Parliament. You can begin to see how easy it might have been for the Lord Mayor of London to recruit all those witnesses to swear to the innocence of the Squires family, for all their smuggling enterprises. Ironically, there was an action replay of the tussle for sunken brandy barrels nearly forty years later, only that time it was between the Customs and the Excise, which were then still two separate services with territories as jealously guarded as any demarcation dispute of later ages.

But if that Abbotsbury squire had a shrewd eye to the main chance (and he wasn't the only one to feel that way about liberated spirits arriving on the local beach), a later Strangways, the 3rd Earl of Ilchester was more sympathetic to the interests of the free traders. When Moses Cousins, the Abbotsbury basket maker whose little cottage still stands in Back Street, was flung into Dorchester Jail for smuggling in 1832, he wrote a pathetic and seriously ungrammatical letter to his landlord the Earl, which led to his release inside a fortnight. Roger Guttridge quotes the letter in full in "Dorset Smugglers" ~

"Me Lord
I have wrote these few lines hoping no ofence from your
lordship in so Doing - thus to say me Moses Cousins
Basket maker Abbotsbury was taken by T. Matts Excise

oficer of abbotsbury with 4 gallons of brandy and as Mr. Foster Vicar and the Gentleman of Abbotsbury has petetiond for amitigation of my imprisonment and has received no answer therefore they has ministered to me to send to your lordship imploring your lordships charitable and humane consideration hoping that as the Gentleman of Abbotsbury will send it if your lordship please to sign it as inever was a smugler before But as trade Being Dull and being introduced to Convey that little quantity of Spirits for the Sake of a few Shillings as times Being hard own to family aflictions That I has been very much reduced in which I solemnly Declare before your lordship that I never was guilty of the like ofence Before in which the Gentleman of Abbotsbury can Certify they never knew me in the Act of Smugling Before till this time and I solemnly Declare never to be guilty of thelike ofence in which iam greatly opressd under the Sentence of mind on the account of the loss of my Business and the sorrowfull Distress of my wife therefore humbly Apeals to your lordships mercy and clemency imploring your lordships charitable and humane consideration of my unhappy case therefore I humbly pray for your lordships favour &c in thus doing iam bound for ever to pray -
I remain your Obedient Servant
Moses Cousins
Dorchester Gaol
Please me Lord to send me Areturn By post at D. Gaol -"

As Roger Guttridge points out, Cousins should have spent a miserable year in prison for failure to pay his £100 fine: it's hardly surprising that he didn't pay, for £100 in 1832 was the equivalent of nearly £5000 today. But his letter paid off: he went in to Dorchester Gaol in December 1832, struggled over his appeal to the Earl on 12 January 1833, and was once more a free man by the 29th of the same month.

By the end of the 19th century, smuggling had had its day, and the last run, in 1882, seems to have been a bit of a disaster: they tried to land at Seatown, and when that failed, they tried every possible port eastwards, failing successively at Eype, Bridport and Burton Bradstock, before managing to beach at Abbotsbury. There was, though, one epilogue, when somebody tried to siphon off some of the Royal Family's wine, intended for their 1947 tour of South Africa, but that, too, was a failure, ending in a substantial fine and a jail sentence. Back in the old days, they could have got out of jail by finding two volunteers each for the Army or the Navy: in those freezing early months of 1947, perhaps jail seemed a warmer option.

Along the rutted track to West Bexington, there are some curiously-named cottages: there's Labour-in-Vain Farm (the bitter opposite of Dunroamin, I suppose), Lawrence's Cottage which has no associations at all with either TE or DH, and a house named after a book. Then, splendidly overlooking the beach after a mile or so stands a terrace of Regency-style clapboard cottages. This is Old Coastguards, built in 1823, just at the time when the Customs service was being overhauled and enlarged to find gainful employment for all the soldiery returning from the Peninsular Wars. Originally housing an inordinate number of officers and their families ~ a figure of 83 people all told is recorded ~ it has for half a century offered a more sybaritic way of watching the coast. When the Coastguard service withdrew from this part of the coast (why does that have a bitterly familiar ring ?), the station was first sold to the novelist HM Tomlinson, who soon after built his own house nearby, calling it *"Gallions Reach"* after the book which had financed his new home.

Even at the height of the tourist season the four cottages, named Matthew, Mark, Luke and John, are never quite as overcrowded as they once were, and the current clientele no doubt enjoy the views just as much as the Bloomsbury aesthetes who gathered here between the wars. Owned, after Tomlinson, by John Middleton Murry, literary critic, essayist and editor of *"The Adelphi"*, (who bought them on an introduction by Thomas Hardy) the cottages played host to everyone who was anyone on the London literary scene: Hardy visited, so did Lawrence of Arabia and Siegfried Sassoon. Murry only had a quarter of the purchase price, but went ahead in hope, and when a royalties cheque for posthumously published work by his first wife arrived in the nick of time, he took it, so it is said, as a blessing from the grave on his second marriage.

Whether JB Priestley called in on the Murry ménage, I don't know, but he liked that end of Abbotsbury and described how *"a turn of the road brought us into Roman Italy. ... We found a carved stone seat at the side of the road, antique Italy in every line and crevice of it, and sat there in the vague trembling sunlight. After that, for the next half mile or so, England disappeared. ... Virgil himself could have passed that ilex-bordered avenue at ease, waiting for the magic of his thunder and tears."*

Eight

Sunlight Again ~ A New Day ?

The question mark in the title of this chapter is important. It's not all that long since influential voices were saying that much needed to be done in Abbotsbury if its beauty and its heritage were not to be lost. Yet those same voices ~ among them the ones that produced the detailed "Appreciation of Abbotsbury" in 1973 ~ left, perhaps deliberately, a lot of ananswered questions.

When this book left the village to head down towards the sea, the note was a little downbeat. Electricity may have arrived, even if it were hidden away, but the sanitary side of life left a lot to be desired by the standards of today's health police. The Earl of the day could still talk of "my people", and those people relied on their Earl. One local lady commented to me that "a lot of fun went out of Abbotsbury when the Honourable John died". Perhaps she was thinking of the traditional Fair on old St Peter's Day, an event about which the pre-war Vicar delicately commented that *"until quite recently the day was marked by some special indulgence in the homes of the villagers. It is said that the discontinuance of the Fair was partly due to the disorders which too often accompanied it"*.

However that may be, even in the postwar years village parents and the Estate alike took it for granted that work and training could be found for every village child; and there was scope enough for work, with the Estate providing its own force of carpenters, painters, plumbers, stonemasons, roofers and thatchers for the village, while the reed beds and withy plantations provided the raw materials for thatch, spars and hurdles (which, of course, needed another work force for their manufacture). In those not-so-long-ago days, the village supported half a dozen or more tenanted farms, each with its own separate work force, but the economy remained basic in our terms, with rents running at 2/6 (12½p) a week, and only occasionally reaching the giddy heights of 6/- (30p). Sounds idyllic until you remember that wages were equally minimal, that as recently as 1972, 80 of the village houses were reported as still having to be connected to the sewers, that buckets for what was, in the municipal euphemism, called night soil were universal, and that water came only from the taps, still visible, built into the fronts of those picturesque high pavements. Mentioning night soil reminds me of the tale in the *Chesil Magazine* of the American soldier billeted here during the war who was asked what he had done with his night soil and replied that he didn't know, as he hadn't been issued with any.

Abbotsbury could easily have declined like so many other rural communities, but for the continuing presence of the Abbey remains and changes to the conservation status of Chesil Beach and the Fleet. By the early 1970s, the dilapidated state of many of the village cottages was already a matter of concern for the Estate. Somehow, it all came together, and a corner was turned. When 1975 was designated Architectural Heritage Year, the village received its reward for its efforts in turning that corner.

The Estate had been gathering its tenanted farms back in to in-house management, and downsizing (though nobody then had thought up such an inhuman term) the work force; that left a number of vacant properties. To its credit, rather than selling them off to the highest bidder and thus forcing the prices beyond local reach, the Estate funded the process of recovery by a combination of converting farm buildings into commercial properties and offering leases to people prepared to modernise rundown cottages at their own expense. Even if Abbotsbury houses command a premium today, the village has thus been spared the common fate of sprawling greenfield development, piecemeal out-of-character infill and astronomically expensive freeholds. Whatever has been built has been carefully blended in to the existing landscape, and for that today's villagers have to thank the remarkable study commissioned by the Estate in 1973, in which every single house is painstakingly described, sometimes with devastating candour.

Twenty-five years after that study, it is interesting to review how much of what was recommended has actually worked out. The invisible "fence" that the study put round the village has not been breached, even by the 1992 development at the Glebe, which has to be a better option than the original one of building between West Street and the Chapel; much of the infill development suggested in 1973 has been carried out, though not necessarily in the way (or in the places) suggested, and the proposed car park has migrated to a totally different site. The underlying philosophy of the study may be grasped from the comment that the roadside walls shouldn't be made too tidy as *"part of their charm lies in their overgrown crumbling appearance"*and the philosophy still holds good today. As to summer holiday traffic, discretion still wins the day and today's highway planners have seen no reason to disagree with the study's verdict that *"this is a knotty problem"*, though it is a problem compounded by locating the huge warning signs for long vehicles joining the road through Abbotsbury from either Weymouth or Bridport just after the last point where it is still possible for a long vehicle to take an alternative route.

~~~~~~~~~~~~~~~~~~~~~~~~~~~~~~~~~~~~~

The Grade II listing of almost every house in the village, the control by leasehold (just as Henry VIII kept Sir Giles in his place 450 years ago), and the existence of an official conservation policy have combined ~ so far, at least ~ to guarantee the integrity of the street scene to this day and ensured that new developments, like the Glebe estate are in keeping with the age-old character of the place. Character is important: Abbotsbury may be a magic place, but it isn't merely a chocolate box showpiece for tourists. The honeypots lie just outside the village, which may be frustrating for those of us whose living depends on visitors, but at least that distance keeps the summertime crowds at a manageable level: or maybe Abbotsbury simply absorbs them, just as it absorbed all those earlier invaders.

Yet, the very success of the place as a tourist attraction raises as many questions as it answers. We'll never again be a declining backwater, but the amount of traffic through the village is about as much as it can take ~ can it be increased without killing off what brings the tourists here ? And can it be cut without threatening the livelihood of those who serve the tourists ? And if that segment of village business goes, will the shops and the Post Office be far behind ?

There has been a steady growth in the number of buildings being turned into art and craft galleries and shops in the village. The first pottery arrived in 1957 and was enlarged in 1973, but of the galleries still operating, Dansel started the conversion trend by taking over what had been an Estate yard in the late 1970s and turning it into a showplace for all kinds of British woodwork. Greg and Lesley Shepherd brought international standards of glass engraving here in the 1980s: Wheelwrights Tea Rooms was once the only place in Britain where Lalique glass could be repaired, and the memory of their stay is kept alive by the life-size figure of wheelwright Sam Mundy on our door, engraved there in 1987.

The self-styled "grandfather of Celtic Art" Courtney Davis lived in the village until recently, Mary Clare Buckle makes jewellery close to where the mediaeval market hall stood, Richard Wilson has been, since 1990, only the latest in a sequence of Abbotsbury potters, while John Varley, John Skinner and Marie Laywine have each totally changed the function of three other traditional village buildings into centres of artistic excellence. Back in 1994, John Skinner inadvertently made press and TV headlines when he placed a life-sized oak carving of a nude, and well-endowed, man outside his studio in Rodden Row. Tongues wagged, and night visitors clothed the figure more than once in nappies, until John turned it round with its back to the street, and buttocks proved less inflammatory.

Meanwhile, here in Wheelwrights, we are gradually feeling our way into a combination of tea and textiles by staging regular exhibitions by contemporary textile artists from as far apart as Falmouth, Oxford and the fringes of London.

Earlier I mentioned Abbotsbury Music: originally launched by local violinist Jean Channon in the early 1980s, the Festival developed further out of a chance meeting between Francesca Radcliffe and visiting singer Marina Tafur in 1989 and an initial series of concerts in the parish church later that year. Ten years on, the Festival's 1999 programme has moved out from the church and into the Gardens, with audiences in their hundreds bringing their picnics (and their anti-midge candle lamps) for evenings of Mozart, flamenco, and Colombian dances, as well as into hands-on children's music sessions in Bridport and a celebration of English music in the very English setting of Sherborne Abbey. But 2000 is the big one: an opera on the theme of St Catherine (she of the Chapel on the hill) especially commissioned, thanks to a Millennium grant, and a project to fill the lady's chapel with banners made by and representing village groups and businesses. Music is also made in the village by the Bridge House Singers, whose concerts are so popular that if you want to sit down for them, you need to be in place 20 minutes before kick-off.

Are all these arts and crafts ventures one way forward ? The crowds who thronged here for Dorset Art Week in 1998 seemed to think so, not least the ones who told us that they had marked the village out as worth a special trip simply because there were half a dozen venues here: that's the equivalent of three stars in a Michelin guide. In 1999, the Abbotsbury artists experimented with our own Arts Week, and managed to lay on nearly 20 exhibitions from one end of the village to the other, in private houses just as much as in professional settings. "One end to the other" is literal, for at one end of the village the Swan Inn hosted an exhibition of children's paintings, which has already proved popular enough to repeat, and Iris Trevett filled her front room with her watercolours (one of which you'll find later in this book), while at the other end, her fellow "Hardy painter" Margaret Sones opened up her garden studio in the last-but one house in the village. An undoubted success, but can the arts and crafts world actually provide regular work for many locals ?

~~~~~~~~~~~~~~~~~~~~~~~~~~~~~~~

The vigour of the Abbotsbury community is also reflected in the monthly *Chesil Magazine* which is distributed for a peppercorn subscription to just about every household in the village by a team of volunteers, just as it is edited and prepared for printing by a dedicated pair of enthusiasts. All the news that's fit to print is there, month after month ~ the old-fashioned grapevine in printed form. And, en passant, we came here from a Devon village expecting to serve our time for twenty years or so before passing the test of acceptance ~ not a chance. On our doorstep when we opened it that first day in 1996, was a greetings card from the butcher, and an invitation to come to a meeting of a proposed association of local businesses. In other respects, too, our welcome to the village was an eye-opener. One competitor after another offered us help in finding us suppliers, putting us on to useful contacts, and inviting us round to their homes. Meanwhile, that proposed association of businesses has blossomed into the Abbotsbury Tourism and Traders Association, with a membership of 25 or more enterprises and a reputation which, we are told by our Business Link contacts, is being held up to our larger neighbours over the ridgeway as something to be copied.

Among the thirty or so businesses around the village, there is a hidden industry in some of these thatched cottages that is wired into the most advanced forms of computer technology: Abbotsbury, for example, is home to the West Dorset Internet. But "The Estate" is still the biggest employer in the village, managing the Gardens, the Swannery and the Tithe Barn, to say nothing of running a flock of 12,000 sheep, farming almost every acre in sight and drawing rents from virtually every property in the village. That adds up to an awesome responsibility, for the welfare of the village hangs entirely on the policies of the Estate. The influence may be a benevolent one, but it needn't always be so, and it isn't everyone in any tourist honeypot who welcomes the annual flood of cars and coaches. Even among those "in the trade", there is a healthy spread of opinion about the style of some of the tourist initiatives that are mooted from time to time.

The jury is still out on one element of the tourist trade here: we had the first hint of what might be in the air when TV's Nick Berry dropped into various village shops and tearooms in the spring of 1998, but it was some time before we heard that filming was in hand for a series based around a local resort. West Bay became Bridehaven, the Bridport Arms doubled up in one colour as the Pier Hotel and in another as the Bridehaven pub (to the confusion of holidaymakers trying to book into a hotel that either didn't exist or masqueraded as two different ones), and the one-time East End barman and later Yorkshire copper changed his name ~ but not his accent ~ to become a Dorset harbourmaster. Hundreds of local folk were signed up as extras ("£30 a day and a free lunch isn't bad for standing round in a crowd" was one verdict), £3 million was pumped in to the local economy, and tourism chiefs talked of similar seven-figure numbers of new visitors flooding in as our area became the latest in a long line of "TV tourism" centres. After the first episode, the commonest comment was that the scenery was the star, and some note seems to have been taken of the second commonest remark, that the citizenry of Bridehaven seemed to have rather more Londoners than locals. Gossip has it, though, that the West Bay car park has been fuller than for many a year.

~~~~~~

Looking back over what I've jotted down in this book, each chapter ~ each break in the mist of the past ~ seems to have had a theme or a motif behind it which I certainly wasn't aware of when I started. The era of the hill fort seemed to be all about the immensely long passages of time that mark out the early history of the valley. The cross-currents of influence from Europe came to the fore when I started to write about the arrival of Danes and Normans among the Saxons (who were themselves immigrants from Germany), while the years when the Benedictines presided over the village spoke of the natural rhythms of seasons and harvests alongside the daily rhythm of work and prayer.

The purchase of the valley by the Strangways family heralded the beginning of one great family making its mark on land and community, while the centuries when nothing much of note seemed to happen were still a period when Abbotsbury people earned their living by the skills of their hands, and the chapters on the parish church, the Gardens, and the surroundings of the Swannery deal with things that are enduring facets of village life for local and visitor alike.

The odd thing is that all of these themes are still alive at the start of the second Christian millennium: we cannot escape the hold that times long past has on the village, we cannot duck the issue of our place on the edge of a Europe with whose rules and customs we don't feel as comfortable as we once did when we could shrug them off as "furriners", while the daily, monthly, yearly, rhythm goes on around us, however differently we mark its movement from the way the Benedictines did.   And, inevitably, the Strangways family, even if no longer resident in the village, still determine a very great deal of what happens here, while the rest of us still earn our crust by using the skills of our hands, our brains and our imagination, just as the monks did.   And we all live daily with the magic of the place, just as the monks did.   Perhaps that's enough for anyone.

References

p. 3   Llewellyn Powys : Dorset Essays - Bodley Head, 1935
p. 8   Coker/Gerard : A Particular Survey of the Countie of Dorset
      (ed. Rodney Legg - Dorset Publishing Company)
p. 9   Roy Strong : The Story of Britain - Pimlico, 1998
"   Coker/Gerard : as above
p.11   Robert Lacey : The Year 1000 - Little, Brown & Co., 1999
"   Opening of King Cnut's charter granting land to Orc, 1024
p.12   Domesday Book : Abbotsbury entry, 1086
p.15   The Rule of St Benedict : in "Documents of the Christian Church",
      (ed. Henry Bettenson © OUP 1963, 1999, by permission of OUP.)
p.16   ibid.
p.18   John Clynn SSF, c.1350
p.20   Rule of St Benedict : as above
p.21   ibid.
"   Proc. of the Dorset Natural History & Archaeological Society, vol 8
p.22   Coker/Gerard : as above
p.23   in Michael Billet : Thatched Buildings of Dorset - Robert Hale
p.26   Dom David Knowles : Religious Orders in England, CUP,1961
p.27   ibid.
"   JR Green : A Short History of the English People - Macmillan, 1875
p.34   Sir John Strangways Account of his Estate in Verse, 1st May, 1650
p.35   Thomas Hardy : A Group of Noble Dames (1891) - Alan Sutton
p.43   Ven. WS Moule : Parish Church guide, 1927
p.44   Elisabeth Green : "The Flight of the Crane" - Epworth Press, 1995
"   Press report : source unknown
p.50   Frederick Treves : Highways & Byways in Dorset, 1906
p.54   Author unknown, c.1909 - Chesil Magazine, 1999
p.57   Brian L Jackson : The Abbotsbury Branch - Wild Swan, 1989
p.61   Kenneth Allsop : In the Country - Hodder, 1972
"   LTS Littman : Ashley Chase - Alan Sutton, 1988
p.64   quoted by Rodney Legg : Literary Dorset - Dorset Publishing Co., 1990
p.65   John Fair : The Mute Swan - Gavin Press, 1985
p.69   LTS Littman : as above
p.71   Llewellyn Powys : Dorset Essays - Bodley Head, 1935
p.75   quoted in Roger Guttridge : Dorset Smugglers - Dorset Pub.Co., 1987
p.78   JB Priestley : The Balconinny and other Essays - Methuen, 1929
p.79   Ven. WS Moule : as above

Illustrations

Acknowledgements

My thanks to the staff at the Record Office, Museum, and Reference Library in Dorchester, and the librarian at Melbury House; but above all to all the Abbotsbury folk who lent me their scrapbooks and told me stories. Anything of interest in this book came from them: anything wrong comes solely from me.

Courtney Davis	Leon & June Edwardes	Dot Ellery
Bill and Madge Ford	Peggy and Henry Ford	Kay Hind
Harold and Betty Hodder	Nell Humpherstone	Joy Langford
Don & Liz Moxom	Colin Roper	Graham Roper
Roger Ross Turner	Betty Ryland	Daphne Sheppard
Tim Snape	Dave Stevens	Reg and Iris Trevett

© Nigel Melville, 1999

Also by Nigel Melville:
"Tidal Range: Ebb and Flow in Appledore"
(Odun Books, 1990)

Odun Books, 14 Rodden Row, Abbotsbury, Dorset DT3 4JL
01305 871800

www.wheelwrights.co.uk

Printed by Creeds, Broadoak, Bridport, Dorset DT6 5NL
01308 423411